MULTINATIONAL INDUSTRIAL RELATIONS SERIES

No. 8. Asian
(No. 8b—I

THE POLITICAL, ECONOMIC, AND LABOR CLIMATE IN INDIA

by

VISWANATHAN VENKATACHALAM

and

RAJIVA K. SINGH

Research Assistants
Industrial Research Unit

INDUSTRIAL RESEARCH UNIT
The Wharton School, Vance Hall/CS
University of Pennsylvania
Philadelphia, Pennsylvania 19104
U.S.A.

331.0954
V461p

c.2

Foreword

In 1972, the Wharton School's Industrial Research Unit established its Multinational Industrial Relations Research Program to supply:

1. key factual information and research concerning the activities, programs, policies, and potential impact of the international unions—including the "trade secretariats," communist and Christian groups, and the regional European, African, and Asian union blocs;

2. similar information regarding the International Labor Organization, the Organization for Economic Cooperation and Development, the United Nations, the European Community's Economic and Social Committee, and other transnational governmental bodies, which frequently are used for and/or support international union objectives and which have adopted codes of conduct for multinational corporations that could significantly affect international labor relations;

3. evaluation of the political, economic, and labor climate affecting investment return in countries throughout the world;

4. analysis and comparison of employee relations and public policy issues among different countries;

5. special in-depth studies, either as part of the research effort concerned with the above or separately underwritten by special information requests.

The publication of this book, *The Political, Economic, and Labor Climate in India,* by Rajiva K. Singh and Viswanathan Venkatachalam, marks the second study of an Asiatic country. In 1980, the Industrial Research Unit published a similar work on the Philippines. One European study—Spain—has been completed, as well as studies of four Latin American countries—Brazil, Mexico, Peru, and Venezuela—and a study of the Arabian Peninsula countries. Studies of Colombia, Nigeria, and a revision of our major study of Brazil are soon to be published or underway.

The authors of this study are both natives of India. Mr. Singh received his bachelor of technology degree at the Indian Institute of Technology, Kanpur, India, and worked in various industrial positions until enrolling in the graduate division of the Wharton School in 1978. He received his master of business administration degree in May 1980, and has since been working for a major United States multinational corporation. During his time at Wharton, he served as a research assistant in the Industrial Research Unit and worked on the project that eventually led to the publication of this book.

Mr. Venkatachalam is currently a candidate for the MBA and MSE degrees at Wharton, and is a native of Madras, India. He was educated at the Indian Institute of Technology, Madras, where he received his bachelor of technology, and at the Indian Institute of Management, Ahmedabad, where he received his postgraduate diploma in management. He worked between 1978 and 1980 as a senior investment analyst for the Liberian Bank for Development and Investment, whose major shareholders are the World Bank (International Finance Corporation) and the government of Liberia. He has also held several positions on the Indian subcontinent, and worked for the Industrial Development and Finance Division of the World Bank in the summer of 1981.

The authors would like to thank the numerous officials at the World Bank, Washington, D.C.; the Embassy of India, Washington, D.C.; the Indian Investment Centre, New York; the Indian Institute of Management, Ahmedabad; and all the other institutions that provided us with important information and access to their documents. This manuscript was edited by Patty Dornbusch, assistant editor of the Industrial Research Unit, and the index was prepared by Mary T. Kiely. Mrs. Margaret E. Doyle handled the various administrative chores involved in the work, and the manuscript was read by several members of the staff of the Industrial Research Unit. The study was financed by contributions of our Multinational Research Advisory Group Information Service subscribers. Such funds are unrestricted, although it is understood that they will be used for multinational industrial relations studies.

The authors are, of course, solely responsible for the study's content and for the research and views expressed, which should not be attributed to the University of Pennsylvania or to the Multinational Research Advisory Group.

HERBERT R. NORTHRUP, *Director*
Industrial Research Unit
The Wharton School
University of Pennsylvania

Philadelphia
April 1982

TABLE OF CONTENTS

LIST OF TABLES

LIST OF FIGURES

CHAPTER I

Introduction

In India, the largest democracy in the world, deeply rooted cultural and social heritages coexist paradoxically with modern technology and radically varied viewpoints. Located in the subcontinent of South Asia, the country has an area of 3,287,782 square kilometers. India became independent in 1947 after nearly 200 years of British rule.

The country's large population and complex social structure make it a unique example of a nation in which the experiment of democracy has been successful despite the presence of diverse languages and incompatible religions. India's adherence to a democratic form of government and to a mixed economy, in which state-owned industries and free enterprise exist together, has had a strong impact on the country's economic climate and labor-management relations. The recently announced shift to an industrial policy that stresses free enterprise is a significant departure from "the Socialistic pattern of society" that was advocated by the late Prime Minister Jawaharlal Nehru and followed by successive governments.

This study investigates the investment climate in India, including its political background and its economic infrastructure. The main focus is on industrial relations and associated legislation. The labor movement in India grew out of the struggle for independence and has been strongly tied to the political parties since its inception. Low wages, high unemployment, and relative lack of education have, however, prevented the movement from achieving the kind of economic power that trade unions in the West have come to exercise. This study traces the development of the Indian labor movement and analyzes issues of importance to the movement, including various labor laws.

Whenever possible, footnotes are provided to substantiate the information presented throughout this text. In some cases, it has been impossible to cite sources because the data are the product of the author's interviews with international labor specialists and businessmen knowledgeable of the region, correspond-

1

ence with Indian unionists, and personal insight. Unfortunately, not all of these sources can be duly acknowledged. Table I-1 provides an informational profile of India.

TABLE I-1
Informational Profile of India

Area	3,287,782 square kilometers, measuring about 3,214 kilometers from south to north between the extreme latitudes and about 2,933 kilometers from east to west between the extreme longitudes.
Population	667 million (1981 estimate). In mid-1975 the average annual growth rate of population was 2.1 percent.
Major Cities	The ten largest cities and their populations (1971—in thousands) are: Calcutta 7,031 Ahmedabad 1,742 Bombay 5,971 Bangalore 1,654 New Delhi 3,647 Kanpur 1,275 Madras 3,170 Poona 1,135 Hyderabad 1,796 Nagpur 930
Religion	Hinduism followed by over 80 percent of population; Islam by about 11 percent; other religions include Christianity, Sikhism, Buddhism, Jainism, Zoroastrianism, and Judaism. Secular state.
Languages	Fifteen major languages, of which English and Hindi are most common. English is the main language for business.
Government	The constitution, promulgated in 1950, provides for a parliamentary, republican, and federal system. The prime minister serves as chief executive with the president as head of state.
Currency	Rupee and Paise. 100 Paise = 1 Rupee (Re.) 1 U.S. $ = 9 Rs. (approximately)
Economy	Predominately agricultural with growing manufacturing and trading sectors. GNP in 1978-79 was Rs. 857 billion (at current prices).
Trade	Total exports of Rs. 57.26 bn (1978-79) and total imports of Rs. 68.14 bn (1978-79). Main exports are jute and textiles, tea, iron ore, leather and leather goods, handicrafts, and engineering goods. Main imports are petroleum, chemicals and fertilizers, iron and steel, and machinery.
Labor force	183 million as of 1974 of which 152 million were male. Expected to expand to 248 million. No current figures of unemployment available but unemployment and underemployment are high.
Measures	Metric system.

CHAPTER II

Politics in India

India attained independence on August 15, 1947, after more than 200 years of British rule. This was the culmination of the peaceful struggle for independence that was conducted mostly by the Indian National Congress. This struggle utilized a new form of political agitation, which was conceived by Mahatma Gandhi and termed "satyagraha," consisting mainly of nonviolent civil disobedience.

Independence, however, was accompanied by the partition of the country into Islamic Pakistan and secular, yet largely Hindu, India. During and after the partition, Hindus and Moslems migrated away from areas in which they were in the minority, creating the largest movement of people known in history. Approximately twelve million people migrated from one country to the other. This movement was accompanied by large-scale communal violence which killed between 500,000 and 1 million people.[1]

THE NEHRU YEARS

Jawaharlal Nehru became the first prime minister of the newly-independent nation. Nehru was a Cambridge-educated lawyer who held liberal socialist views. He led a Congress Party cabinet of ministers and oversaw the creation of a constitution that went into effect on January 26, 1950.[2] The formulators of the constitution extracted features that were suitable for India from various Western models and produced a synthesized version. Thus, the parliamentary form of government was of British origin while the emphasis on the fundamental rights of citizens came from the American model.

---

[1] Richard F. Nyrop et al., *Area Handbook for India* (Washington, D.C.: U.S. Government Printing Office, 1975), pp. 46-47.

[2] *India: A Reference Annual, 1979* (New Delhi: Publications Division, Ministry of Information and Broadcasting, Government of India, 1979), p. 17.

3

The constitution created a "sovereign democratic republic," and stressed justice, freedom, and equality. All citizens were to enjoy social, economic, and political justice, and have freedom of thought, expression, belief, faith, and worship. Equality was given in status, opportunity, and law. Certain fundamental rights were guaranteed, such as freedom of religion, culture, speech, and assembly. The constitution also established directive principles of state policy as guidelines for efforts of the nation. These principles urged legislative and executive action to bring about improvements in a wide variety of issues such as village organization, living standards, benefits, education, backward [i.e., underprivileged] classes, and the civil code.

Nehru, a Westernized, liberal democrat, pursued policies of large-scale industrial development, agrarian reforms, social elevation of the untouchables, national integration, and education for the masses. He implemented his policies through the legislative and administrative provisions of the constitution and the efficient infrastructure of civil servants that the British had left behind. Nehru launched a series of ambitious five-year development plans, and the economy made significant progress in the first ten years of Indian independence, but population problems and a lack of fiscal reforms impeded achievement of the plans' desired results.

Nehru played a vigorous role in the international sphere by providing leadership to the newly emerging Third World nations and maintaining a truly nonaligned status in the bipolar political environment of the 1950s and early 1960s. His growing international prestige suffered a setback because of India's poor military performance in the border conflict with China in 1962. Two years later, Nehru died after ruling the country for fifteen years.

India's political organization is profiled in Table II-1.

POST-NEHRU INDIA

Lal Bahadur Shastri, Nehru's successor as prime minister, continued the nonaligned links forged by Nehru. His initial achievements were mending fences with neighboring countries and making peace between various factions within the country. India, however, will remember Shastri for the firmness and determination he showed in the border conflict with Pakistan in August and September of 1965. India's forces performed well in the field

TABLE II-1
India's Political Organization

Structure	India is a sovereign, democratic republic with a parliamentary system of government. The nation is a federation of twenty-two states and is governed under the terms of the constitution of India which came into force on January 26, 1950.
Administration	The president of India is the constitutional head of the union and the supreme commander of its armed forces. He is assisted by the prime minister and the cabinet. The executive power, therefore, is in the hands of the prime minister, who is also the leader of the majority group in the Lok Sabha (House of the People or lower house). The states are similarly governed by chief ministers under the state head, the governor, or appointees of the president. The jurisdictions of the state and the union are clearly demarcated by the constitution. The executive, legislative, and judiciary systems are independent of each other.
	The union comprises twenty-two states and nine union territories. The states are: Andhra Pradesh, Assam, Bihar, Gujarat, Haryana, Himachal Pradesh, Jammu and Kashmir, Karnataka, Kerala, Madhya Pradesh, Maharashtra, Manipur, Meghalaya, Nagaland, Orissa, Punjab, Rajasthan, Sikkim, Tamil Nadu, Tripura, Uttar Pradesh, and West Bengal. The union territories are: Andaman and Nicobar Islands, Arunachal Pradesh, Chandigarh, Dadra and Nacar Haveli, Delhi, Goa, Daman and Diu, Lakshadweep, Mizoram, and Pondicherry.
Official Language	Hindi, in Devnagari script, is the official language of the union. Under the Official Language Act, 1963, English will continue to be used along with Hindi. English is used widely in the business sector.
Legislative System	The legislature of the union, called the Parliament, consists of the president and two houses. Lok Sabha (House of the People), or the lower house, consists of 544 members who are directly elected from the 22 states and the 9 union territories. Rajya Sabha (House of the State), or the upper house, has 244 members; 231 are indirectly elected and represent the states and the union territories; one is nominated by the president to represent the union territory of Arunachal Pradesh; the remaining 12 members are nominated by the president to represent art, literature, sciences, and social service.
	All legislation requires the consent of both houses of Parliament. The Parliament also has the power to amend the constitution.

TABLE II-1 (Continued)

Judiciary	The Indian constitution seeks to ensure the independence of the judiciary. The Supreme Court of India consists of a chief justice and thirteen other judges appointed by the president. The Supreme Court has original and appellate jurisdiction. Disputes between states, and between states and the union fall under its original jurisdiction in regard to the enforcement of fundamental rights. The Supreme Court has appellate jurisdiction over the high court of the states in both civil and criminal cases involving substantial questions concerning the interpretation of the law.
International Organizations	India is a member of the United Nations and most of its affiliated organizations. It is also a member of the Commonwealth of Nations and the Colombo Plan.

Source: *India: A Reference Annual, 1979* (New Delhi: Publications Division, Ministry of Information and Broadcasting, Government of India, 1979), pp. 17-38.

against Pakistan's, and this helped to restore India's national pride. A combined effort of the United States and the Soviet Union brought about a cease-fire on September 23, 1965, which was followed by a Soviet-sponsored settlement in Tashkent in January 1966. The settlement called for both countries to withdraw to the positions they held before the fighting began; both India and Pakistan complied. Shastri died in Tashkent soon after the settlement.[3]

The post-Nehru era, however, has been dominated by his even more powerful daughter, Mrs. Indira Gandhi, who was elected on a trial basis and who later took complete control of the Congress Party and the country's political life. Her first three years in power were ridden with political chaos on the state level, and civil disturbances took place throughout the nation. The Congress Party, under Mrs. Gandhi's leadership, reached its political nadir in the 1967 general elections with a drastically reduced majority in Parliament. She retained the premiership, but the conservative "bosses" of the Congress Party continued to exert political pressure on Mrs. Gandhi.

Mrs. Gandhi, however, with considerable political acumen, detached herself from the party bosses, who were known as the

[3] Nyrop et al., *Area Handbook*, p. 52.

"syndicate," and formed her own party with a majority of the Congress Party's membership in the Parliament; this new party became known as the Congress (I) Party. Feeling the pulse of the masses, she commenced a program of socialist economic policies, including such major acts as the nationalization of the nation's fourteen largest banks and the symbolic abolition of special privileges for the ex-rulers of princely states.

Mrs. Gandhi strengthened her tenuous majority in the Parliament by calling for general elections in December 1970, a year ahead of schedule, banking on her populist political stand and the public's impatience with chaotic, unstable state governments. Mrs. Gandhi's Congress (I) won a landslide victory of 350 out of 521 seats in the Lok Sabha (lower house of Parliament), giving her the power to secure the passage of constitutional amendments. With her firm and capable handling of the East Pakistan crisis, which led to the formation of Bangladesh, her personal prestige and political power reached an all-time high.

In 1975, deepening economic crisis and increasing political opposition to Mrs. Gandhi's rule were beginning to loosen her grip on power in India; then, as a result of an unfair electoral practice suit, the Allahabad High Court unseated her from Parliament on relatively minor technical and legal grounds in June 1975. Mrs. Gandhi countered this threat to her position and attempted to control the growing political, industrial, and civil disorder by declaring a state of internal emergency and suspending fundamental rights and civil liberties. Thousands, including opposition leaders, labor union officials, and political dissenters, were imprisoned almost overnight under the broad constitutional powers with which the state of emergency provided the government.

The state of emergency had a positive impact on the economy and industrial relations. Investments improved as a result of the stable industrial climate, and productivity increased as a result of the forcibly improved labor conditions. Helped by good harvests and a better balance of payments, the economy improved. The country, however, was witnessing protests against massive repression, bureaucratic abuse, and the growing extraconstitutional influence of Mrs. Gandhi's younger son, Sanjay Gandhi. Disagreement with the government was widespread. Assessing the situation inaccurately, Mrs. Gandhi called for general elections to the Parliament in January 1977.

Contrary to her expectations, she lost the elections, and stepped down quietly, refuting the predictions of many observers that democracy was premature in the Third World.[4]

The newly formed Janata Party, an incohesive group consisting of the old Congress Party, the Jan Sangh, the Socialist Party, and others of various political ideologies common only in their opposition to Mrs. Gandhi, came to power in March 1977. The revival of the country's democratic political life was, however, accompanied by the kind of civil indiscipline that existed before Mrs. Gandhi's emergency rule. The economy, industrial life, and the labor situation began to deteriorate under the government of the new prime minister, Morarji Desai. The two and a half years of the Janata Party's rule were indifferent to the country's desperate need for development, primarily because the party leaders took contradictory policy directions in accordance with their diverse political ideologies.

The political differences between various factions of the Janata Party led to the breakup of the party into Janata and Janata (secular). The Janata (secular) faction, headed by Desai's one-time deputy prime minister and finance minister, Charan Singh, withdrew its support of Desai's government. This resulted in Desai's resignation as prime minister on July 15, 1979. In a shrewd political move, the Congress (I) Party, led by former Prime Minister Indira Gandhi, supported Charan Singh's bid for prime ministership, and Mr. Singh was named India's prime minister on July 26, 1979. The new government, composed of several political groups with no common political ideology, started out on unstable grounds. Four weeks later, on the eve of a no-confidence vote in the Parliament, Mrs. Gandhi withdrew her support of Charan Singh's government, thus forcing him to resign. The president dissolved the Parliament and called for new national elections. Frustrated by the poor economic performances of the Desai and Singh governments, the deteriorating law and order situation, and the general lack of direction in the country, the electorate voted strongly in favor of Mrs. Gandhi's Congress (I) Party in elections held in the first week of January 1980. Mrs. Gandhi's Congress (I) Party won a two-thirds majority in the Parliament and Mrs. Gandhi became the new prime minister.

---

[4] Myron Weiner, *India at the Polls: The Parliamentary Elections of 1977* (Washington, D.C.: American Enterprise Institute for Public Policy Research, 1978), p. 1.

This development was expected in a large number of domestic and international circles to lead to more stability and better economic conditions in India. Mrs. Gandhi's party, however, greatly lacked the kind of capable people needed to overcome India's growing economic and social ills; and the party was dominated by a young, inexperienced, and ideologically uncertain group of people handpicked by Gandhi's son, Sanjay, who was also elected to the Parliament. Even though Mrs. Gandhi gave him no government office, Sanjay's dominance of the party machinery and the government gave him the status of heir apparent to prime ministership. Sanjay Gandhi and his young supporters moved the Congress Party to the right and favored a more balanced relationship between the public sector and free enterprise.

Sanjay Gandhi's death in an airplane crash on June 23, 1980, changed the entire political equation and led to uncertainty about the future of Mrs. Gandhi's government. Mrs. Gandhi has already proved to thrive on adversity, and it is likely that she will maintain her strong control of the party and the government. But the factionalism within the party probably will grow, and rivalry between the party veterans and the younger members will probably intensify as both groups struggle to fill the void left by the death of the most powerful figure in the party. Mrs. Gandhi's ability to balance the demands of competing factions will determine, to a large extent, the political future of India. Mrs. Gandhi is, however, expected to continue the right-wing thrust that was initiated by her son in the area of economic policy making.

POLITICAL PARTIES

Since independence, hundreds of parties of many political ideologies, regional loyalties, and religious biases have emerged in India. Most of them have been local in nature and brief in existence, merging into like-minded parties or disbanding due to lack of popular support. The political arena, however, is still clouded by a plethora of parties, and the realignments and shifting loyalties make the evolution of the party structure that exists today confusing to all but the most seasoned and close observers of Indian politics.

The Indian National Congress (INC), formed in 1885 during the days of British colonialism, was the mainstay of Indian politics through the first four general elections held after independence. The INC was founded and nurtured by stalwarts, and it commanded a degree of national eminence and awe hardly approached by any party today. The primary reason for the cohesiveness of the INC was its common goal of independence; after independence was achieved in 1947, factionalism and power struggles grew within the Congress. A section of the INC that held socialist ideals left the party and formed the Socialist Party, which later split into the Samyukta Socialist Party (SSP) and the Praja Socialist Party (PSP).

The major split in the INC occurred in 1969 when Mrs. Indira Gandhi broke with the conservative faction of that party. As prime minister, Mrs. Gandhi followed a socialist program that emphasized development of the public sector over the private sector; she also sought a greater role for the state in the monetary, industrial, and commercial sectors of the economy. Her faction was initially called Congress (Ruling) or Congress (R) and was later called Congress (Indira) or Congress (I). The other faction, which was controlled by the conservative leaders, was called Congress (Organization) or Congress (O).

Mrs. Gandhi's party suffered another split in 1978 when it broke into two groups, Congress (I) and Congress (Reddy), named after its president—Reddy. The Congress (I) lost blood again when one of Mrs. Gandhi's major supporters, Devraj Urs, left the party to join the Congress (Reddy) group. Later, Urs became president of the Congress (Reddy) party, which henceforth was called Congress (U). (Figure II-1 shows the various realignments of the Indian political system between 1969 and 1980.) In the 1980 elections, however, the Congress (I) won a resounding victory with 351 seats while the Congress (U) obtained only 13 seats.

The Congress (Organization), until it merged with the Janata Party in 1977, was controlled by the conservatives. The party supported a mixed economy and opposed state capitalism. It stood for the protection of private property, the guarantee of fundamental constitutional rights, and the independence of the judiciary.

The Swatantra Party, founded in 1959, stood for greater freedom for expansion of private enterprise, the strengthening of peasant proprietorship, fewer government controls, a "rational" tax system, and incentives for greater production. This party was the second largest opposition party in the Lok Sabha, winning forty-four seats in the general elections of 1967. It was reduced to seventh largest, with only eight seats, as a result of

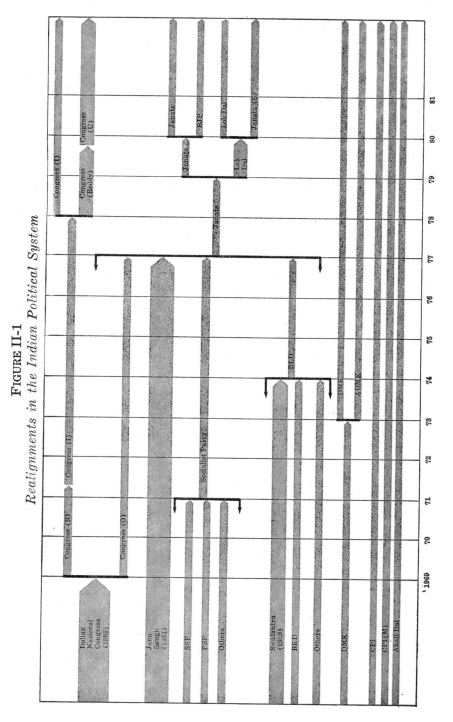

FIGURE II-1

Realignments in the Indian Political System

the 1971 elections (see Table II-2), and merged with the Bhartiya Lok Dal in 1974.

The Jan Sangh, formed in 1951, was committed to a nationalist, pro-Hindu ideology, supporting fundamental property rights and opposing state interference in trade and industry. This party was particularly strong in northern India, where it participated in five coalition state governments after 1967. While the Jan Sangh won only thirty-five seats in the Parliament in 1967 and twenty-two in 1971, it appeared to be gaining popularity after 1971. The Jan Sangh merged with the Janata Party in 1977.

The Bhartiya Lok Dal (BLD) was formed by the merger of seven small, regional parties in 1974. The most important of these were the Bhartiya Kranti Dal (BKD) and the Swatantra Party. The Swatantra Party was supported by the more prosperous farmers of Uttar Pradesh and businessmen and landlords of Rajasthan and Orissa. The BLD merged with the Janata Party in 1977.

The Socialist Party of India (SPI) was formed in 1971 as a result of the merger of the Samyukta Socialist Party, the Praja Socialist Party, and some other socialist groups. Their ideologies incorporated Marxist, Gandhian, and democratic socialist philosophies. The SPI supported nationalization of foreign companies, ceilings on landholdings, and an equitable distribution of the nation's wealth. It was one of the four major parties which merged to form the Janata Party in 1977.

The Janata Party, the ruling party until July 1979, was formed under the chairmanship of Morarji Desai in 1977 to offer a national alternative to Mrs. Gandhi's Congress Party. The Janata Party was formed by the merger of the Jan Sangh, the Socialist Party, the Bhartiya Lok Dal, and the Congress (Organization). It won 298 seats in the Parliament in 1977 out of a total of 539. The Janata Party was an ideologically disparate combination of politicians with almost all shades of political thought. Internal political strains led to a political crisis in July 1979, when the Bhartiya Lok Dal and the Socialist members of the Janata formed a new party by the name of Lok Dal.

The Janata Party had weakened considerably and won only 32 seats out of 525 in the 1980 elections. The Lok Dal fared better and obtained forty-one seats. Dissensions in both parties grew, however, and a few months after the elections, the Janata Party split into the Janata Party and the Bhartiya Janata Party

TABLE II-2
Lok Sabha Elections: 1952—1980

Party	1952 No. of Seats	1952 % of Votes	1957 No. of Seats	1957 % of Votes	1962 No. of Seats	1962 % of Votes	1967 No. of Seats	1967 % of Votes	1971 No. of Seats	1971 % of Votes	1977 No. of Seats	1977 % of Votes	1980 No. of Seats	1980 % of Votes
Indian National Congress	364	44.99	371	47.78	361	44.73	283	40.73	—	—	—	—	—	—
Congress (I)	—	—	—	—	—	—	—	—	352	43.6	153	34.5	351	—
Congress (O)	—	—	—	—	—	—	—	—	16	10.4	—	—	—	—
Congress (U)	—	—	—	—	—	—	—	—	—	—	—	—	13	—
Janata	—	—	—	—	—	—	—	—	—	—	298	43.2	32	—
Lok Dal	—	—	—	—	—	—	—	—	—	—	—	—	41	—
Jan Sangh	3	3.06	4	5.93	14	6.44	35	9.41	22	7.4	—	—	—	—
Swatantra	—	—	—	—	18	7.89	44	8.68	8	3.1	—	—	—	—
Praja Socialist Party	—	—	19	10.41	12	6.81	13	3.06	2	1.03	—	—	—	—
Samyukta Socialist Party	—	—	—	—	—	—	23	4.92	3	2.44	—	—	—	—
Republican Party	—	—	—	—	—	—	1	2.48	—	—	—	—	—	—
Communist Party of India	16	3.29	27	8.92	29	9.94	23	5.19	23	4.9	7	2.8	10	—
Communist Party of India/Marxist	—	—	—	—	—	—	19	4.21	25	5.1	21	4.2	35	—
Others & Independents	106	48.66	73	26.96	60	21.36	79	21.32	39	15.3	60	15.2	43	—
TOTAL	489	100.00	494	100.00	494	100.00	520	100.00	518	100.00	539	100.00	525	—

Source: Surinder Suri, *Politics and Society in India* (Calcutta: Naya Prokash, 1974), p. 312. Myron Weiner, *India at the Polls: The Parliamentary Elections of 1977* (Washington, D.C.: American Enterprise Institute for Public Policy Research, 1978), p. 68.
"Indira's Landslide Win Brightens Prospects for Stability in India," *Business Asia*, Vol. XII, No. 2 (January 11, 1980), p. 12.

(BJP). Another group, led by Raj Narain, left the Lok Dal and formed the Janata (Secular), or Janata (S), Party.

The Communist Party of India (CPI) and the Communist Party of India/Marxist (CPI/M) have been politically significant only at the state level, even though they held twenty-three and twenty-five seats, respectively, in the Parliament after the 1971 elections (see Table II-2). The two parties ruled the states of West Bengal and Kerala, either separately or together, for some time. The CPI supported Mrs. Gandhi's pro-left policies and backed her in the 1977 elections, while the CPI/M opposed her policies and, hence, supported the Janata. With seven and twenty-one seats respectively, however, the CPI and CPI/M suffered major losses in the 1977 elections; they fared a bit better in the 1980 elections, winning ten and thirty-five seats respectively.

Other regional parties, like the Akali Dal of Punjab, the Dravid Munnetra Kazhagam (DMK), and the rival Anna Dravid Munnetra Kazhagam (ADMK) of Tamil Nadu, also aligned themselves with one of the national parties during elections. During 1971, the DMK supported Mrs. Gandhi, but after a DMK government was dismissed on corruption charges during Mrs. Gandhi's emergency rule, it supported the Janata in the 1977 elections. The DMK changed its policy later and supported Mrs. Gandhi again in the 1980 elections. The ADMK aligned itself with Mrs. Gandhi in 1977 but supported the Janata in the 1980 elections.

Shifting loyalties, infighting, and power-plays have dominated the Indian political scene since the last three general elections. Given India's poverty, unemployment, and illiteracy, it is doubtful whether political moves with popular appeal and politics based on personalities will give way in the foreseeable future to a mature political structure based on sound social, economic, and political philosophies.

FOREIGN POLICY

Jawaharlal Nehru, who served as foreign minister as well as prime minister from 1947 until his death in 1964, was the main architect of India's foreign policy. He advocated nonalignment, peaceful coexistence, and mutual respect for territorial integrity as the basis of international relations. India followed a genuine nonalignment policy until 1971, when it signed a twenty-year treaty of friendship and cooperation with the Soviet Union.[5] This

---

[5] Nyrop et al., *Area Handbook*, p. 381.

treaty does not call for a military alliance, but is interpreted as ensuring mutual support in the face of military threats by a third party. The treaty provides a much needed means of reassurance in view of India's increasing diplomatic isolation from Pakistan and China. India's major diplomatic problems have been related to its border disputes with Pakistan and China; these disputes resulted in wars with Pakistan in 1947-48, 1965, and 1971 and with China in 1962. India's dispute with Pakistan over the state of Kashmir, which both India and Pakistan claim as theirs, has made it impossible for the countries to have good relations. The creation of Bangladesh from East Pakistan as a result of India's 1971 war with Pakistan and the emergence of India as a dominant regional power have forced Pakistan to accept the status quo on Kashmir, at least temporarily, and the new governments are making efforts toward a more harmonious relationship. Pakistan's attempts to acquire a nuclear capability equal to India's and Indian anxieties about such attempts have aroused deep suspicions in both countries. The relationship between these two countries is likely to remain troubled until a satisfactory solution to the Kashmir issue is found.

India's relations with the Soviet Union have improved from the cool response the Soviets gave to India's policies immediately after independence to closer and extremely cordial relations in the recent past. Both countries cultivated close relations with a number of reciprocatory visits by their leaders. The Soviet Union's endorsement of India's stand on Kashmir and Goa, and Pakistan's alliance in September 1954 with the western countries in the Southeast Asia Treaty Organization (SEATO) brought India closer to the Soviet Union. The growing influence of the Soviet Union on India helped bring peace to the subcontinent after the August 1965 war between India and Pakistan. Mrs. Gandhi's government realized in 1971 that the country faced a war with Pakistan on the Bangladesh issue and that China, and possibly even the United States, would help Pakistan in the war. So, in August 1971, India signed the twenty-year treaty of friendship and cooperation with the Soviet Union. This treaty changed the political relationship of the two countries, bringing them even closer. The change of government in March 1977 did not change Indo-Soviet relations, and with Mrs. Gandhi's return to power in 1980, the Indo-Soviet relationship is certain to remain close.

India's relations with the United States have been central to its foreign policy since independence. The American support of India's struggle for independence created a great amount of goodwill between the countries. India also studied the American constitutional democratic system and built a number of its features into its own system. Being the two largest democracies in the world, India and the United States have a background of common policies. Even with a background of overall agreements, however, there have been areas of major disagreement between the two countries, and both have overemphasized these differences in the formulation of their foreign policy toward each other.

India did not accept the United States' policy of anticommunism and chose to remain nonaligned. It also disagreed with the United States' policy of not recognizing the People's Republic of China, and of approving regional defense pacts like the Central Treaty Organization (CENTO) and SEATO. The United States' policy of regional balance of power led it to support Pakistan by supplying it with arms, and this caused bitterness on India's part.

Despite political differences, the United States has participated widely in economic and technical aid to India. It has also supplied India with millions of tons of food grains to alleviate food shortages there from time to time. The United States also helped India during the 1962 border conflict with China by supplying arms and openly supporting India. This, however, was during the Kennedy administration when relations between the two countries were at their best. The differences increased later on due to India's criticism of United States involvement in Vietnam and United States support of Pakistan when Pakistan was also deriving support from China. The relationship between India and the United States reached its nadir during the Nixon presidency when Nixon continued to support Pakistan and ordered the S.S. Enterprise of the Seventh Fleet into the Bay of Bengal as a token show of support to Pakistan during the Bangladesh War. United States rapprochement with China further exacerbated the relations between India and the United States.

The change of governments in both Washington and New Delhi in 1977 healed these relations a little. President Carter's acceptance of India's importance and his politically important trip to India in January 1978 helped to restore relations between the two countries.

With the rise to power again of Mrs. Gandhi in the 1980 elections, with her strong Soviet tilt, and with the Reagan administration's cautious policy toward the Soviets, India and the United States are unlikely to become closer. Differences remain between the countries, especially over India's refusal to sign the nuclear nonproliferation treaty, and America's refusal to supply India with enriched nuclear fuel for its power plants. Furthermore, India's noncondemnation of Soviet intervention in Afghanistan, its recognition of the Heng Samrin regime in Kampuchea, its growing dependence on the Soviet Union for trade, and its vigorous opposition to the American naval base in Diego Garcia in the Indian Ocean have not endeared it to the United States.

Similarly, India views with concern the Reagan administration's proposals to reduce aid packages around the globe; even more alarming to India is the recently announced five-year $3.2 billion military and economic assistance package to Pakistan, India's traditional enemy. Thus, relations between India and the United States are unlikely to improve further unless some basic attitudinal changes take place first.

CHAPTER III

The Indian Economy in Profile

The Indian economy continues to be predominantly agricultural, with about half of the country's national income derived from agricultural and allied activities and three-fourths of its work force employed by the agricultural sector. The industrial sector has received national attention and planning resources only in the last thirty years. A lack of economic direction in several successive governments and an ideological adherence to a mixed economic structure have been major obstacles to rapid economic development in India. Poor economic resources and a rapidly growing population have also weakened the impact of national economic planning. The situation has been aggravated by increasing inflation resulting from food shortages and the devastating effect of oil price increases on India's petroleum imports. The economic discipline brought on by Mrs. Gandhi's emergency rule had a positive effect on general economic conditions. After her electoral defeat in 1977, the new government allowed the economy to decline and severe inflationary conditions resulted. After her return to power in January 1980, conditions improved somewhat, but the long-term prospects for the country depend on the government's willingness to put economic pragmatism before political ideology.

India's economic growth since independence has, however, been significant given the economic conditions at the time of its birth. A sophisticated national planning system using a series of five-year plans has been the principal force behind the economic development effort. The plans have been aimed at balancing growth in the industrial and agricultural sectors and increasing equity of distribution of wealth; they have had only limited success so far.

ECONOMIC PLANNING

The directive principles of state policy set forth in the constitution are the guideposts for economic planning in India. The

economy is viewed as composed of two complementary sectors:
the public sector and the private sector. All government-owned
organizations are classified under the public sector, and all
privately-owned organizations under the private sector. The
government has had three main objectives in its planning process: self-sustained economic growth, reduction of inequality, and
a socialist pattern of society—even though changes in priority
have occurred from time to time.

The idea of a mixed economy for independent India gained
popularity after the worldwide depression in the 1930s, when
the Indian National Congress adopted it as the official party
policy. The party formed a planning committee under the chairmanship of Jawaharlal Nehru in 1937 to prepare a comprehensive economic plan for the country.[1] Nehru and his party were
primarily responsible for formulating the ideological basis of
Indian economic planning, which was termed "democratic social-
ism." The planning process in India was inspired by the Russian five-year plans, but it differed from the Russian pattern in
its recognition of the importance of private enterprise, and in
its execution. Some observers have found this combination both
paradoxical and unique.[2]

In April 1948, the Indian government announced its policy for
the future industrial development of the country.[3] The policy
outlined the government's intention to control the key nationally
important industries, especially the heavy industries. This set
the pattern, which continues to date, of increased state participation in industries. To coordinate the economic planning process,
the government set up the Planning Commission in 1950. The
prime minister is the chairman of the commission, and is assisted
by economists and civil servants. The Planning Commission has
formulated six five-year plans since its inception; these are de-
scribed below.

The First Five-Year Plan—1951-1956

The first plan sought to initiate rapid development of basic
resources and to correct the economic disequilibrium caused by

---

[1] Braj Kishor and B. P. Singh, *Indian Economy Through the Plans* (New
Delhi: National Publishing House, 1969), p. 106.

[2] Charles Bettelheim, *India Independent* (New York: Monthly Review
Press, 1968), p. 147.

[3] Dhires Bhattacharyya, *India's Five Year Plans* (Calcutta: Progressive
Publishers, 1975), p. 44.

the Second World War and the partition. Agriculture, irrigation, and power projects were accorded the highest priority. About 44.6 percent of the total outlay for the public sector, which was Rs. 20.69 billion, was allocated to these projects. The plan also aimed at increasing the rate of investment from 5 percent to about 7 percent of national income.[4] Because the plan was limited in scope, its success was greater than expected. National income, which had been targeted to increase by 11 percent, rose to 15.5 percent above the level of 1950-51. The ratio of investment to income moved up by 8 percent in five years as compared with the targeted increase of 6.75 percent. The industrial production index in 1955-56 was 40 percent higher than it was in 1950-51.[5] This was partly due, however, to better utilization of already established capacity, and not to an increase in capacity. The apparent success of the plan was undermined by lagging investment in sectors of the economy critical to future growth, including power, steel, and fertilizers, and also by slackened financial resource mobilization and increasing budgetary deficits.

The Second Five-Year Plan—1956-1961

The second five-year plan, besides being more ambitious than the first, was also guided by a new political objective. In 1954, the Indian Parliament adopted a resolution accepting the goal of "a socialist pattern of society" as a guiding principle of national economic policy. This policy was formalized by means of a revised industrial policy in 1956 that reserved for the state a large sector of industry and aimed at higher growth for the public sector.

The main aims of the second plan were to increase the national income by 25 percent, promote rapid industrialization, especially the development of basic and heavy industries, expand employment opportunities, reduce inequalities in income and wealth, and effect a more even distribution of economic power. The plan was also aimed at increasing the rate of investment from about 7 percent of the national income to 11 percent by 1961. Total outlays of Rs. 48 billion for the public sector and Rs. 24 billion for

---

[4] *India: A Reference Annual, 1979* (New Delhi: Publications Division, Ministry of Information and Broadcasting, Government of India, 1979), p. 199.

[5] Bhattacharyya, *India's Five Year Plans*, p. 57.

the private sector were proposed. The distribution of the outlays is shown in Table III-1.

TABLE III-1
Distribution of Plan Outlay by Major Heads of Development
(in Billions of Rs.)

	First Plan Total Provision	%	Second Plan Total Provision	%
Agricultural and Community Development	3.57	15	5.68	12
Irrigation and Flood Control	4.01	17	4.86	10
Power	2.60	11	4.27	9
Industries and Minerals	1.79	7	8.90	18
Transport and Communications	5.57	24	13.85	29
Social Services, Housing, and Rehabilitation	5.33	23	9.45	20
Miscellaneous	.69	3	.99	2
TOTAL:	23.56	100	48.00	100

Source: Braj Kishor and B. P. Singh, *Indian Economy through the Plans*
(New Delhi: National Publishing House, 1969), p. 139.

The shifting allocations for each segment of the national economy show that the priorities of the government changed. The
second plan was heavily biased toward heavy industry and
mining, for which the allocation was increased from 7 percent of
the total in the first five-year plan to 18 percent in the second.
The agricultural sector, the allocation of which was scaled down
from 15 to 12 percent, suffered the most, with the situation
aggravated by bad climatic conditions in the second half of the
1950s. Transport and communications accounted for about 29
percent of the total outlay. Some 19 percent of the total outlay
was devoted to irrigation and power. Social services took up
about 20 percent of the total outlay in the second plan as compared with 23 percent in the first plan. The actual outlay, however, had variations that reflected, to a large extent, the capacity
and willingness of the economy to be guided by the plan. The
actual total outlay was Rs. 2 billion less than had been planned,
and the reduction was reflected in all segments except power and
industries, as shown in Table III-2.

Considering that the real value of investments during the second plan was not rising as fast as money figures indicate, the growth rate during the second plan was satisfactory. Investments as a proportion of national income increased from about 7.5 percent at the close of the first plan to over 11 percent at the close of the second plan.

The savings rate increased only by 9 percent, from 7.6 percent to 8.5 percent. The gap between investments and savings had to be financed by drawing down sterling balances and external capital. National income increased by nearly 20 percent against a target of 25 percent. But considering the constraints of capital formation and an overly-optimistic assumption of capital-output ratio, this performance was not bad. The second plan placed greater emphasis on capital-intensive projects that had longer gestation periods, and therefore the short-term projects did not perform as well. The per capita income increased by 8 percent, and this could have been greater but for the higher-than-expected population increase of 10.3 percent.[6]

In terms of production in various sectors of the economy, the plan was indeed successful. Agricultural as well as industrial

TABLE III-2

Distribution of Outlay: Second Plan

	Planned		Actual	
	Outlay (billion Rs.)	Percentage	Expenditure (billion Rs.)	Percentage
Agricultural and Community Development	5.68	12	5.30	11
Irrigation and Flood Control	4.86	10	4.20	9
Power	4.27	9	4.45	10
Industries and Minerals	8.90	18	9.00	20
Transport and Communications	13.85	29	13.00	28
Social Service and Miscellaneous	10.44	22	10.05	22
TOTAL:	48.00	100	46.00	100

Source: Kishor and Singh, *Indian Economy Through the Plans*, p. 140.

---

[6] Kishor and Singh, *Indian Economy Through the Plans*, p. 142.

production showed significant gains. Table III-3 shows the production increases for various industries.

TABLE III-3
*Selected Indicators of Economic Progress
During the Second Plan Period*

	Unit	Production in 1955-66	Production in 1960-61
Foodgrains	million tons	66.9	82.0
Cotton Cloth (mills)	million tons	4665	4649
Sugar	million tons	1.9	3.0
Paper and Board	thousand tons	190	350
Steel (finished)	million tons	1.3	2.4
Cement	million tons	4.7	8.0
Nitrogenous Fertilizers	thousand tons	80	99
Phosphatic Fertilizers	thousand tons	12	54
Coal	million tons	39.0	55.5
Electricity Generation	million kwh.	10,777	20,023

Source: Dhires Bhattacharyya, *India's Five Year Plans* (Calcutta: Progressive Publishers, 1975), p. 72.

Industrial production during the second plan increased by 41 percent as compared with 39 percent during the first plan, while the increase in agricultural production remained the same, at 22 percent.[7] Major growth occurred in steel and machine-building industries, and significant progress occurred in consumer products industries. Power generation increased significantly in the same period. The installed capacity of hydroelectric power increased from 0.56 million Kw to 1.93 million Kw, and that of thermal power increased from 1.74 million Kw to 3.77 million Kw during the decade.[8] Although this increase was impressive, it fell substantially short of the target of 6.9 million Kw.

The overall achievements of the second plan were undermined by the difficulties faced in financing it, as well as by the problem of food shortages. The gap between investment and savings led to excessive dependence on foreign aid, and domestic prices increased by an annual rate of 6 percent during the period. It was during this period that the Indian economy entered the vicious

---

[7] Bhattacharyya, *India's Five Year Plans*, p. 73.

[8] Kishor and Singh, *Indian Economy Through the Plans*, p. 146.

circle of deficit financing, further taxation, and resulting price increases, in which it is still entangled.

The Third Five-Year Plan—1961-1966

The broad strategy of the third plan was to carry forward the task undertaken in the first two plans and correct the imbalances in national economic planning. Development of the agricultural sector received special emphasis in view of the food problems faced in the earlier plan period. The need to import food grains was recognized as detrimental to other developmental imports.

The plan was aimed at securing self-sustained growth by increasing both investment and savings. The rate of domestic savings was projected to increase from 8.5 percent to 11.5 percent of the national income and the rate of investment from 11 percent to about 15 percent of the national income. To realize these broad goals, the plan's immediate objectives were to secure an increase in the national income of over 5 percent per annum, achieve self-sufficiency in foodgrains, expand basic industries, utilize manpower resources efficiently and reduce disparities in income and wealth.

The national income was projected to increase by about 30 percent from Rs. 145 billion in 1960-61 to about Rs. 190 billion by 1965-66 (at 1960-61 price), and per capita income by about 17 percent from Rs. 330 to Rs. 385 during the same period. A total outlay of Rs. 75 billion was proposed for the public sector and Rs. 41 billion for the private sector. The plan thus provided for an increase of about 54 percent in total investment—70 percent in the public sector and 32 percent in the private sector.[9] A breakdown of the plan by sectors is shown in Table III-4.

The plan fell short of the targeted growth in agriculture, industry, and national income. The actual outlay was Rs. 85.77 billion, substantially higher than the targeted outlay of Rs. 75 billion, but no benefits were derived from this excess expenditure. This was explained only partly by the severe downturn in agricultural production that was caused by unfavorable climatic conditions in 1965-66. The national income rose by less than 20 percent against a target of 23 percent. Per capita income changed very little between 1960-61 and 1965-66 because the 2.5

---

[9] *Ibid.* pp. 153-154.

TABLE III-4
Investment in Second and Third Plans
(billions Rs.)

	Second Plan		Third Plan			
	Total (Public & Private)	Percentage	Public	Private	Total	Percentage
Agricultural and Community Development	8.35	12	6.60	8.00	14.60	14
Major and Medium Irrigation	4.20	6	6.50	*	6.50	6
Power	4.85	7	10.12	.50	10.62	10
Organized Industry and Minerals	15.45	23	15.20	10.50	25.70	25
Village and Small Industries	2.65	4	9.50	2.75	4.25	4
Transport and Communications	14.10	21	14.86	2.50	17.36	17
Social Services and Misc.	12.90	19	6.22	10.75	16.97	16
Inventories	5.00	8	2.00	6.00	8.00	8
TOTAL:	67.50	100	63.00	41.00 **	104.00	100

* Included under agricultural and community development.
** Excludes transfers from public to private sector.
Source: *The Third Five-Year Plan* (New Delhi: Government of India, Planning Commission, 1961), p. 59.

percent annual rate of population growth cancelled out the meager growth in national income.[10]

The performance of the third plan was thus ineffective. Between 1950-51 and 1960-61 the industrial output had expanded 96 percent and agricultural output 49 percent, while during the third plan period, industrial output increased by 50 percent and agricultural output by only 12.5 percent (leaving out the unfavorable agricultural year of 1965-66). These declines were responsible for the development of shortages and the increased demand for imports which created formidable balance of payments problems. Although the output of major consumer goods did not increase remarkably, as shown by Table III-5, the steel, aluminum, and machine-tool industries showed increases of 200 percent to 300 percent in output.[11]

TABLE III-5

Increase in Output of Major Consumer Goods Between 1960-61 and 1964-65

Commodity	Unit	Output in 1960-61	Output in 1964-65
Foodgrains	million tons	82.0	89.36
Mill Cloth	million meters	4649.0	4675.00
Sugar	million tons	2.7	2.90
Vegetable Oils	thousand tons	340.0	366.00
Paper and Board	thousand tons	350.0	493.00

Source: Bhattacharyya, *India's Five Year Plans*, p. 82.

While the third plan was considered unsuccessful in quantitative terms, it did produce qualitative benefits, such as acceptance of the concept of balanced regional development in the national planning process, improvement in the structural factors of the economy, and generation of a national consciousness in attaining economic welfare through democratic planning.

The Annual Plans—1966-1969

The diversion of resources from development efforts to defense spending because of the 1965 war with Pakistan and the virtual stoppage of foreign economic assistance came at a time when

---

[10] *Ibid.*, p. 156.

[11] Bhattacharyya, *India's Five Year Plans*, pp. 80-82.

India's external balance position was becoming increasingly worse. The rupee was devalued in June 1966 and a decision was taken by the government to defer the fourth five-year plan until the economic situation became normal. The government formulated annual plans to guide the development expenditure that was possible with the reduced resources. This period of the annual plans, 1966 through 1969, is also referred to as a "Plan Holiday" period.

In the three years of annual plans, the public sector development outlay amounted to Rs. 66.25 billion. The sectoral allocation of such development expenditure is shown in Table III-6.

TABLE III-6

Allocation of Public Sector Development Outlay, 1966-1969
(billion Rs.)

Item of Outlay	1966-67	1967-68	1968-69	Total During 1968-69	Percentage of Total Outlay
Agriculture and Community Development	3.34	3.14	4.39 *	11.07	17.0
Irrigation and Power	5.53	5.41	5.89	16.83	25.0
Industry and Mining	5.57	5.13	5.66	16.83	24.0
Transport and Communications	4.24	3.98	4.01	12.23	20.0
Social Services	2.69	2.90	3.25	8.84	13.0
Other Programs	.27	.29	.36	.92	1.0
	21.64	20.85	23.76	66.25	100.0

* Includes provision for buffer stocks.
Source: Bhattacharyya, *India's Five Year Plans*, p. 85.

As can be observed from the table, the major thrust of the annual plans was to continue existing projects, hence there were no major shifts from the earlier plans. Private sector growth was inhibited during this period, mainly because of the devaluation of the rupee in 1966, which increased the rupee cost of imports substantially, and because of the government's lack of economic direction. Growth of industrial output fell to 12 percent over these three years as compared to 48 percent over the third plan period.

The recession in the majority of industries and the poor performance of the agricultural sector created a severe setback for the growth of national and per capita income. The five-year plan system was reinstated in 1969 amid the expectations of a large group of people who had been bypassed by the benefits of the annual planning process.

The Fourth Five-Year Plan—1969-1974

At the end of the third five-year plan period, there had been widespread realization in the country that the planning process had benefited only a small sector of the economy. Constantly increasing prices denied any gains to the vast majority of the people on fixed incomes. A reconstituted Planning Commission was given the task of redefining the objectives of planning and reworking priorities, with the primary aim of bringing the benefits of planning to all classes of people in the country. The major stresses in the fourth five-year plan were on self-reliance and increasing the effectiveness of development across various sectors of the economy.

The targeted overall outlay for the fourth plan was Rs. 248.82 billion with Rs. 159.02 billion allocated to the public sector and Rs. 89.80 billion allocated to the private sector. The total investment was thus to be divided between the public and private sectors in a ratio of about 3:2. The distribution of the outlay for the public sector is shown in Table III-7.

TABLE III-7

Distribution of Plan Outlay in the Public Sector:
The Fourth Plan 1969-74

Type of Outlay	Amount (billions Rs.)	Percentage
Agricultural and Allied Sectors	27.28	17.2
Irrigation and Power	35.34	22.2
Industry and Mining	36.31	22.8
Transport and Communications	32.37	20.4
Social Services	25.80	16.2
Others	1.92	1.2
	159.02	100.0

Source: *Statistical Outline of India* (Bombay: Tata Services Limited, 1978), p. 172.

Compared to the third five-year plan, the fourth plan gave a higher priority to the agricultural and social services sectors, while lowering the proportions outlaid to transport and communications. The shares of resources given to irrigation power and industries were kept at their earlier levels.

The targeted rate of growth in national income for the fourth plan, 5.5 percent per year, was expected to provide for a growth in per capita income of 3 percent per year. The national income, at 1968-69 prices, was expected to increase from Rs. 288.00 billion in 1968-69 to Rs. 379.00 billion in 1973-74. Per capita annual income was targeted to rise from Rs. 545 to Rs. 636 during the same period. Besides the objective of growth, the plan was aimed at reducing interregional disparities and large-scale unemployment. By reducing food imports and increasing exports, the plan was aimed at reducing need for foreign aid. To achieve these goals, net investment had to move up from 11.2 percent of national income in 1968-69 to 14.5 percent by the end of the plan period.[12] A substantial increase in the savings rate was projected to finance this from domestic resources.

The plan had limited success in the agricultural and transportation sectors, but the results in the industrial sector were below the targets. The industrial sector suffered from both lack of capacity utilization and failure to achieve the targeted rates of increase in investment. Severe supply bottlenecks caused by faulty planning, haphazard coordination, and decreased demand were two major reasons for the failure of the plan in the industrial sector. The plan also failed to curb inflation.

The Fifth Five-Year Plan—1974-1979

The main problems that the fourth plan set out to tackle, such as unemployment and widespread poverty, remained unsolved at the end of the plan period, and severe inflationary trends continued. The fifth five-year plan attempted to overcome these problems in a bold realignment of priorities. The plan was aimed at equalizing availability of such basic needs as primary education, medical care, roads, communication, and drinking water. The projects in the fifth plan were chosen to generate greater employment opportunities without unnecessary sacrifice of long-term growth objectives. The plan was to adopt measures for raising the consumption standards of people living below the

---

[12] *Ibid.*, p. 95.

poverty line. This was to be achieved by suitable measures of taxation and subsidies and by developing a system of public distribution of essential consumer goods at fair prices. The plan also gave high priority to bringing inflation under control and to achieving stability in the economic situation.

The fifth plan projected an outlay of Rs. 663.53 billion, of which the public sector outlay was Rs. 393.04 billion and the expected private investment was Rs. 270.49 billion.[13] The distribution of funds for the fifth plan is given in Table III-8.

Like the fourth plan, the fifth plan had an inauspicious start. Severe domestic inflation followed the crop failures of 1971-72 and 1972-73, and an inordinate expansion of the money supply caused a severe resource crisis. The high inflation rate rendered the plan figures relatively meaningless. The aggregate growth rate, targeted at 4.37 percent, was only 3.9 percent in the first four years of the plan period.[14] It was then decided to end the five-year plan a year early and initiate work on a new plan for the next five years with new priorities and new programs.

TABLE III-8

Distribution of Plan Outlay in the Public Sector:
The Fifth Five-Year Plan, 1974-79

Type of Outlay	Amount (billion Rs.)	Percentage
Agriculture and Allied Sectors	46.44	11.8
Irrigation	34.40	8.8
Power	72.94	18.6
Industry and Mining	102.21	26.0
Transport and Communication	68.81	17.5
Social Services	68.28	17.4
Others	—	—
TOTAL:	393.08	100.0

Source: *Statistical Outline of India*, 1978, p. 172.

The Sixth Five-Year Plan—1980-1985

The change in government in March 1977 and the resultant shift in economic policy were reflected in the draft sixth plan published in March 1978. The objectives of self-reliance, removal

---

[13] *India: A Reference Annual, 1979*, p. 201.

[14] *Quarterly Economic Review of India, Nepal*, Annual Supplement 1979, The Economist Intelligence Unit, p. 20.

of unemployment, and greater equality of economic welfare were
retained. In addition, agricultural and rural outlays were increased substantially over those in the fifth plan. The sixth plan
was intended to be more flexible than its predecessor and was
based on the principle of annual rolling plans. The draft sixth
plan set an average growth target of 4.8 percent. The plan,
however, was not put into action when the Janata Party was in
power, and national economic planning during that time was
conducted on an annual basis.

With Mrs. Gandhi's reelection in 1980, the sixth plan was
revised. The rolling plan concept initiated by the Janata Party
was discarded. In February 1981, the National Development Coun-
cil approved the sixth plan (1980-85). The main goal of the
plan is to reduce the percentage of the population that is below
the poverty line from 48 percent to 30 percent. A growth rate
of 5.2 percent per annum through an investment of Rs. 1,772
billion is projected, with the public sector receiving a slightly
greater share of the total investment. Per capita income is
projected to grow at 3.3 percent per annum. The plan empha-
sizes self-reliance through speedy development of the economy
and a reduction in foreign aid. Employment is expected to increase from 151 million standard person years to 185 million
standard person years.[15]

In retrospect, the economic planning process in India has had
achievements along with some notable failures. The plans have
helped the country develop an impressive infrastructure of irrigation reservoirs, dams, modern steel and fertilizer plants, machine-building capacity, power-generating capacity, and a fairly
advanced educational system. The vast population of India, however, has failed to gain any benefits from the plans due to their
narrow focus and poor fiscal and monetary policies, as well as to
unfavorable climatic conditions in several years, and the unex-
pected diversion of national resources to three wars with China
and Pakistan. In view of the fast-growing population and its
consumption and employment needs, a vast effort is required.
Despite the failure of the plans on several fronts, one thing
remains certain: the economic planning process initiated by
Nehru is likely to govern to a large extent the economic directions, investment climate, and industrial and agricultural pros-
perity of the country.

---

15 "Sixth plan cleared: 5.2 percent growth rate," *The Overseas Hindustan
Times*, February 26, 1981, p. 4.

INFRASTRUCTURE

One of the main achievements of the five-year plans has been progress in developing an impressive infrastructure for industry, transportation, commerce, and communications. Major gains have been made in production capacities for steel, cement, power generation, chemicals, and fertilizers. As a result of planned development, roads, railways, aviation, and shipping transport sectors have showed large improvements. The major thrust of the five-year plans has been to develop the infrastructure for future growth while maintaining, and hopefully increasing, current growth rates.

Railways

The Indian railway system is the largest in Asia and the fourth largest in the world. The system, which is state-owned, has a route length of 60,666 kilometers and carries over 9 million passengers and 0.6 million tons of freight a year. About 11,000 trains run everyday, and 7,083 train stations are in operation. Most industrial and commercial sectors are well served by railways, and the operational fleet consists of 11,010 locomotives, 36,794 passenger coaches, and 397,773 freight wagons. Railway employees number about 1.5 million, the total investment is around Rs. 55.72 billion, and revenues are about Rs. 20.36 billion. Since 1951, both passenger and freight traffic have more than doubled. While the number of passenger vehicles and wagons has practically doubled, the number of locomotives has increased by only 34 percent.[16]

Railway routes in India have increased continually. There has also been a move toward modernization of track and conversion to electric locomotives. Table III-9 shows the progress of the system between 1950 and 1977. Electrified route length has increased more than twelvefold since 1950. Electric and diesel locomotives are gradually replacing steam locomotives. The pace of modernization must be accelerated, however, if the system is to efficiently serve the increasing demand for its services.

Roads

The Indian road network has grown significantly in the last thirty years. The total road length currently is estimated at 1.375

---

[16] *India: A Reference Annual, 1979*, p. 344.

TABLE III-9
Progress of Government Railways

Year	Route length (kilometers) Elec- trified	Non- Elec- trified	Total	Running Track (km)	Passen- gers Origi- nating (million)	Goods Origi- nating (million tons)
1950-51	388	53,208	53,596	59,315	1,284.0	93.0
1960-61	748	55,499	56,247	63,602	1,594.0	156.2
1965-66	2,423	55,976	58,399	68,375	2,082.0	203.0
1970-71	3,706	56,084	59,790	71,669	2,431.1	196.5
1971-72	3,953	56,115	60,067	73,225	2,535.8	197.8
1972-73	4,055	56,094	60,149	73,664	2,653.0	201.3
1973-74	4,191	56,043	60,234	74,104	2,643.7	184.9
1974-75	4,397	55,904	60,301	74,197	2,429.0	196.6
1975-76	4,649	—	60,216	74,255	2,945.2	223.3
1976-77	4,719	55,947	60,666	74,839	3,300.3	239.1

Source: *India: A Reference Annual 1979* (New Delhi: Publications Division, Ministry of Information and Broadcasting, Government of India), p. 344.

million kilometers compared with 0.4 million kilometers in 1950. The five-year plans allocated major sums to development and improvement of the road network. The total number of motor vehicles on roads in March 1977 was 2.937 million, nearly thirteen times the number in 1947. This included 1.217 million motor-cycles, 0.728 million private cars and jeeps, 0.191 million public service vehicles, and 0.371 million goods vehicles. Passenger traffic has been nationalized in most states whereas goods freight transport continues to be almost exclusively in the private sector. The number of passenger vehicles in the public sector during the last 10 years has increased from 28,000 to over 56,000 and there has been persistent demand for increased services, particularly in metropolitan areas. The state transport system services over 27 million commuters every day, and the industry employs about 400,000 persons.[17]

Table III-10 shows the kilometers of roads constructed during selected years since 1951.

Inland Waterways

India has about 5,200 kilometers of major rivers that are navigable by power craft, but only 1,700 kilometers are actually

[17] *Ibid.*, p. 352.

used. The total length of canals is 4,300 kilometers, but only 485 kilometers are suitable for power craft, and only 331 kilometers are actually being used.

The major navigable waterways are the Ganges, the Brahmaputra, and their tributaries—the Godavari, the Krishna, the Mahanadi, the Narmada, and the Tapti, and their canals; the backwaters and the canals of Kerala, the Buckingham Canal in Andhra Pradesh and Tamil Nadu and the Cumbarjua Canal connecting the Mandovi and the Zuvari Rivers in Goa.[18]

Shipping and Ports

India has the second largest fleet of ships in Asia and ranks sixteenth in the world in terms of tonnage. Indian ships operate on most of the sea routes of the world. Even though coastal shipping plays only a minor role in India, the merchant fleet for international trade has grown rapidly and is fast approaching 6 million gross registered tons.[19] Figure III-1 illustrates the growth of shipping in India in the last thirty years.

Half of India's liner cargo and almost all of its oil is carried on Indian ships; only bulk cargo, such as iron ore bound for Japan is still transported predominantly by foreign ships. Indian shipping was badly harmed by the slump of the mid-1970s, but with the recent rise in freight rates, the fleet is operating without losses. The growth of Indian shipping was helped by the government's development fund, which provided up to 90 percent of the cost of new vessels through loans at a concessional rate of interest. The government, however, expects the shipping companies to pay a larger share of the cost of future vessels; this and other factors are likely to slow the expansion of the fleet.

TABLE III-10

Progress of Road Construction 1950-51 to 1975-76
(in thousands of kilometers)

Type of Road	1950-51	1960-61	1971-72	1972-73	1973-74	1974-75	1975-76
Surfaced	157	263	423	449	475	484	533
Unsurfaced	243	261	599	627	663	706	843
TOTAL	400	524	1,022	1,076	1,138	1,190	1,376

Source: *India: A Reference Annual, 1979*, p. 350.

---

[18] *Ibid.*, p. 353.

[19] "India on the Move," *The Economist*, March 8, 1980, p. 109.

FIGURE III-1
Growth of Shipping in India

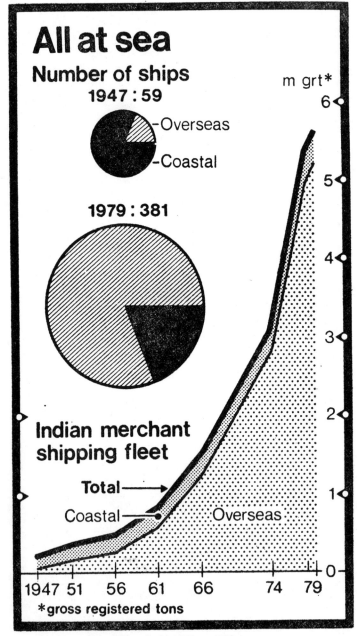

Source: *The Economist,* March 8, 1980, p. 109.

Currently, there are fifty shipping companies in the country. Two of these, the Shipping Corporation of India, Ltd. (SCI) and the Mogul Line, Ltd., are in the public sector and the rest are in the private sector. India is a signatory of the United Nations code of conduct for liner companies.

India has 10 major ports and over 160 intermediate and minor ports scattered along its 6,100 kilometers of coastline. Bombay is the largest and most active port with about a quarter of India's foreign trade passing through it. Calcutta, on the east coast, is the largest terminal port in South Asia. It is supplemented by the new mechanized dock system, with provision for deeper draughted vessels, at the nearby port of Haldia. Other major ports are in Cochin, Kandla, Madras, Mormugao, Paradip, Vishakhapatnam, Mangalore, and Tuticorin. Figures for the years 1976-77 show that the major ports handled 677 million tons of freight in that year.

Aviation

After the Second World War, surplus aircraft were utilized for commercial purposes, and civil aviation in India was born. At the time of independence, eleven airlines were operating. These were nationalized in 1943 into two public sector corporations; Air India for international travel, and Indian Airlines for domestic traffic and neighboring countries. The passenger traffic of Indian Airlines has increased almost twentyfold since 1947 to an estimated 5.5 million persons per year. Air cargo, however, is insignificant, amounting to barely 50,000 tons per year.[20] Air India provides service to thirty-four countries. During 1976, it carried 862,661 passengers and flew about 652 million ton-kilometers of cargo.[21]

The Civil Aviation Directorate operates all civil airports except international airports. It is also responsible for the air navigation services for safety and regularity of aircraft operations. About eighty-five airports are maintained by the directorate. The four international airports, which are at Bombay, Calcutta, New Delhi, and Madras, are operated by the International Airports Authority of India. The country and its major cities are thus easily accessible by air.

---

[20] *Ibid.*

[21] *India: A Reference Annual, 1979*, p. 361.

Communications

The country has made remarkable progress in communication
services since independence, but the infrastructure is backward
by Western standards. Since independence, the number of post
offices has more than tripled, the number of telegraph offices more
than doubled, and the number of telephones increased elevenfold.

Postal and communications services are provided by the Posts
and Telegraph Board. In April 1977, there were 120,999 post
offices, of which 108,491 were in rural areas. Each post office
served an average of 4,533 persons and served an area of 27.17
square kilometers. The value of postal articles handled during
1975-76 was Rs. 7.40 billion with revenues of Rs. 1.67 billion.[22]
Telegraph services consist of over 19,000 telegraph offices and
conventional telex and teleprinter services that are available for
commercial and industrial use. Telex services are available between seventy cities and have a total installed capacity of 16,720
connections.

The telephone came into use in India soon after its invention,
with the first exchange established in Calcutta as early as 1881.
By 1947, India had 321 exchanges with 86,000 telephones. Rapid
advances have been made since then, and currently there are
over 2 million telephones. Demand for telephones is high, however, and the waiting period in some cities can be several years.
Automatic trunk dialing is now in operation on all major routes.
India's external telecommunications services are operated by the
Overseas Communications Service (OCS) from its headquarters
in Bombay. The OCS operates through four international gate-
way centers, located in Bombay, Calcutta, Madras, and New
Delhi, and provides overseas telegraph, telephone, telex, radio-
photo, and leased telegraph channel services. Most major cities
worldwide are accessible through telecommunications, but the
service is less than satisfactory.

The OCS leases teleprinter channels for the exclusive use of
private subscribers. Several international airlines, foreign em-
bassies, and international business houses use these facilities.

Audio and video broadcasting are government-controlled, with
All-India Radio overseeing radio broadcasts and "Doordarshan"
overseeing television. All-India Radio has eighty-two stations,
which cover the entire nation. Commercial advertising was in-

---

[22] *Ibid.*, p. 367.

troduced on the national radio system in 1968 and is now available in most parts of the country.

Television is still in the early stages of development with only black-and-white transmissions. Currently, eight television stations are operating in India at New Delhi, Bombay, Calcutta, Madras, Srinagar, Amritsar, Lucknow, and Ahmedabad. The sixth five-year plan has approved proposals for three new television stations, to be located at Jaipur, Trivandrum, and Bangalore, with several relay stations around the country. Commercial advertisement facilities are available at most centers.

The press is one of the most important media of communication in India, with a total of 13,320 newspapers. The largest number of newspapers are published in Hindi, followed by English and Urdu; smaller numbers of papers are published in other regional languages. Total circulation of all daily newspapers in 1976 was 34 million.

Although by Western standards the media and communication systems in India are not fully developed, the progress made in the last thirty years is indeed impressive. Greater expenditure of capital and more planning would be necessary, however, to bring the overall quality and quantity of telecommunications facilities into line with the needs of the growing economy.

Energy

Coal, oil, hydropower, and thermal power provide energy for India's commercial needs. Firewood and organic wastes, the noncommercial sources of energy, provide energy for most of the rural dwellers. India imports 65 percent of its oil requirements. The sharp increases in oil prices in October 1973 affected India severely. The value of imported crude oil went up from Rs. 3.33 billion in 1973 to Rs. 28 billion in 1979 with serious repercussions for India's balance of payments.[23] Measures have been introduced to curb consumption of petroleum products and to substitute other energy sources for petroleum. Recognition of the importance of energy to overall economic growth and of the need for a coordinated approach to the development of various energy forms led to the creation of the Ministry of Energy in October 1974.

---

[23] K. K. Sharma, "Oil imports becoming an impossible burden," *Financial Times*, March 17, 1980, p. XXIII.

Power development has been given a high priority in the development programs because of its crucial role in all economic sectors. Despite its early beginning, hydroelectric power did not progress significantly in India until 1947. The installed capacity then was as low as 1.9 million kw, concentrated mainly around urban centers. Power generation programs made phenomenal progress with the advent of the five-year plans, however, and current power generating capacity is about 29,000 mw, of which 10,000 mw is hydropower, 16,000 mw thermal power, 640 mw nuclear power, and 2,200 mw from other sources.[24] Figure III-2 shows the growth of installed capacity and generation between 1947 and 1977.

Coal has been gaining importance as a source of energy since the petroleum price hikes of 1973. Proven coal reserves in India are more than 85 billion tons, a quarter of which is of coking quality.[25] Indian coal production has risen from 32 million tons in 1950 to well over 100 million tons per year at present.[26]

Coal production in India is now almost completely in the public sector, organized mainly by Coal India, Limited, through its subsidiary companies. Investment of Rs. 2 billion in the mines by the government raised the output to about 100 million tons, at which level it has stagnated for the last five years. Demand, however, has been increasing at about 12 percent a year and severe power shortages have resulted. This has had disastrous effects in industrial and agricultural production, and growth rates in 1979 and 1980 were lower than those of 1978. An urgent program of mechanization, efficient transportation, and increased investment in this sector are thus needed to stimulate economic growth as a whole.

India's per capita oil consumption is one of the lowest in the world, although its total consumption is roughly 30 million tons a year. Roughly a third of the oil consumed in India is produced in oil-fields in the northeast, in Gujrat, and in offshore sites on the western continental shelf. The remaining oil is imported primarily from the Middle East. India's oil imports easily constitute the single largest item in the import bill, and

[24] *Quarterly Economic Review of India, Nepal,* Annual Supplement 1979, p. 12.

[25] David Dodwell, "Coal reserves are vital," *Financial Times,* March 17, 1980, p. XIV.

[26] *India: A Reference Annual, 1979,* p. 280.

FIGURE III-2

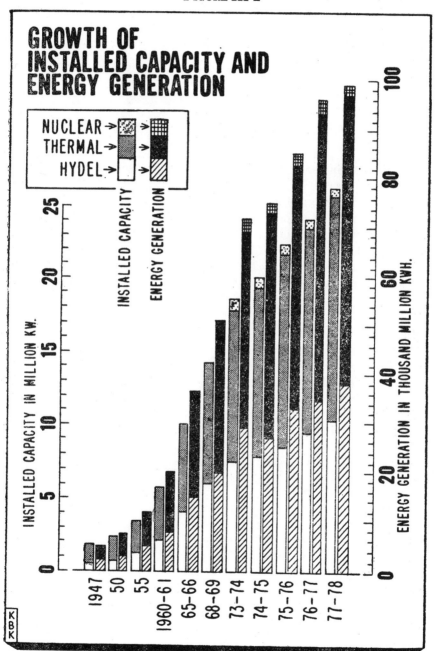

a substantial portion of export earnings must be used to pay for oil imports. The government has recently increased efforts to raise domestic production of oil by giving exploration and drilling for oil a major share of public sector investment, as well as by inviting foreign oil companies to participate in joint exploratory ventures. Provisional figures indicate that reserves of crude oil number 310.37 million tons, and that those of natural gas number 238.74 million cubic meters.[27]

INDUSTRY

The industrial sector in India has progressed rapidly in the last thirty years. The five-year plans provided the infrastructure and capacity for large, capital-intensive industries, and a strong entrepreneurial class contributed to the development of diverse industries of various other sizes. The industrial sector in India is governed by the policies of the Ministry of Industry. The private sector is heavily regulated, and this has been a major obstacle to greater industrial development of the country.

Industrial Policy and Licensing

Independent India's industrial policy was first announced in 1948. This policy called for a mixed economy with the government taking overall responsibility for planning the development and regulation of industries. The policy was revised in 1956, and certain industries were declared either schedule A or schedule B industries. Schedule A industries were to be henceforth the exclusive domain of the state, while schedule B industries were to be progressively state-owned. Industries not specified in either schedule were to be developed by the private sector, with the government nevertheless retaining the freedom to enter them at its discretion. The industries specified in Schedules A and B consist mainly of basic and heavy industries that provide major inputs to other industries, especially to industries of military significance.

The Industries Development and Regulation Act, 1951 is the primary legislative act governing the establishment and regulation of industries in India. Under the act, an industrial license is required to establish a new undertaking or to expand an industry listed in the act. The government can exempt certain

---

[27] K. K. Sharma, "Oil imports becoming an impossible burden," *Financial Times*, March 17, 1980, p. XXIII.

industries from the provisions of the act at its discretion; at present, small scale and ancillary units enjoy this exemption (see Appendix A). Further, undertakings with assets of greater than Rs. 200 million can enter only certain industries, as specified in the act (see Appendix B). They can enter other industries provided that at least 60 percent of the new or additional production will be exported (to be achieved within three years); entry into industries reserved for the small-scale sector requires that at least 75 percent of the new or additional production be exported.

The policy for international investments in Indian industry is also governed by the act and is discussed in the section of this chapter entitled Foreign Investment.

Principal Industries

Iron and Steel. The first major efforts at large-scale iron and steel production were undertaken when the Tata Iron and Steel Company (TISCO) was set up at Jamshedpur in 1907. In 1919, the Indian Iron and Steel Company (IISCO) was established at Burnpur. The first company in the public sector, now known as the Visvesvaraya Iron and Steel Works, Ltd., started operating at Bhadravati in 1923. After independence, a major effort was directed at developing the iron and steel industry in the public sector. There are, at present, six integrated steel plants in the country, four in the public sector, and two in the private sector. The management of the Indian Iron and Steel Company, a private-sector plant, was taken over by the central government in 1972. Table III-11 shows the capacity of the six integrated steel plants.

TABLE III-11

Production Capacity of the Six Integrated Steel Plants in India
(in thousands of tons)

Plant	Ingot Steel	Saleable Steel
Public Sector		
Bhilai	2,500	1,965
Durgapur	1,600	1,239
Rourkela	1,800	1,225
Bokaro	1,700	1,355
IISCO	1,000	800
Private Sector		
TISCO	2,000	1,500
TOTAL:	10,600	8,084

Source: *India: A Reference Annual, 1979*, p. 307.

Engineering Industries. The engineering industries in India were started after independence and have grown significantly since then. Not only has India become self-reliant in the manufacture of a variety of kinds of engineering equipment, but it has also succeeded in exporting equipment to several countries. The country is currently producing equipment for generating, transmitting, and distributing power, machinery for production of steel, chemicals, and fertilizers, electrical and construction machinery, machine tools, agricultural equipment, and a large number of other items (see Table III-12).

In 1976-77, the engineering industries produced goods worth over Rs. 40 billion. The progress made over the years is indeed remarkable, as the output of the light and medium industries in 1950-51 was only Rs. 500 million. Export of engineering goods in 1976-77 reached an all time high of Rs. 5.52 billion, as compared to Rs. 60 million in 1950-51.

Chemicals and Fertilizers. Two petrochemical complexes, one owned by Union Carbide India Ltd., and the other by National Organic Chemicals Ltd., started production in 1967 and 1968, respectively. To speed the establishment of petrochemical complexes around the public-sector refineries, the Indian Petrochemicals Corporation Ltd. (IPCL) was set up in 1969 in the public sector. Production of plastics in the country was 102,801 tons in 1976. Synthetic fiber production was 48,151 tons and synthetic rubber production was 28,359 tons in 1977. [28]

The fertilizer industry, in view of its importance to agricultural development, has been given special encouragement through the plans. At the time of independence, the industry consisted of only a few plants manufacturing single superphosphate and ammonium sulphate as a by-product of smelter gases. The first large-sized plant for the manufacture of nitrogenous fertilizers was established at Alwaye, in Kerala, in 1947. Another large plant in the public sector went into production at Sindri in October 1951. The industry has made rapid strides since then. Capacity has increased from 85,000 tons of nitrogen and 63,500 tons of superphosphate in 1951-52 to 3.26 million tons of nitrogen and 1.08 million tons of superphosphate at the end of 1976-77.[29] Over the years, India has also developed considerable expertise in the design, engineering, erection, commissioning, and operation of

---

[28] *India: A Reference Annual, 1979,* p. 314.

[29] *Ibid.,* p. 314.

TABLE III-12

Progress of Industrial Production (Selected Industries)

Industry (Unit)	1950-51	1960-61	1965-66	1970-71	1975-76	1976-77	1977-78
I. Mining							
1. Coal (including lignite) (a)	32.8	55.7	70.3	74.3	102.7	104.8	104.7
2. Iron ore (a)	3.0	11.0	18.1	22.5	42.2	42.4	41.0
II. Metallurgical Industries							
3. Pig iron (a)	1.69	4.31	7.09	6.99	8.55	10.06	9.51
4. Steel Ingots (a)	1.47	3.42	6.53	6.14	7.48	8.66	8.64
5. Saleable steel (a)	1.04	2.39	4.51	4.48	5.92	7.06	7.02
6. Steel castings (b)	—	34	57	62	61.9	63.2	66.0
7. Aluminum (virgin metal) (b)	4	18.3	62.1	166.8	187.3	208.7	178.5
8. Copper (virgin metal) (b)	7.1	8.5	9.4	9.3	23.9	23.7	21.1
III. Mechanical Engineering Industries							
9. Machine tools (c)	3	70	294	430	1141	1163	1027
10. Railway wagons (d)	2.9	11.9	33.5	11.1	12.2	12.0	12.2
11. Automobiles (d)	16.5	55	70.7	87.4	72.7	91.3	83.9
(i) Commercial vehicles (d)	8.6	28.4	35.3	41.2	43.8	46.4	40.9
(ii) Passenger cars etc. (d)	7.9	26.6	35.4	46.2	21.8	36.5	33.9
12. Motorcycles and scooters (d)	—	19.4	40.7	97.0	182.4	228.9	225.2
13. Power driven pumps (d)	35	109	224	259	274	309	352
14. Diesel engines (stationary) (d)	5.5	44.7	93.1	65.7	137.6	111.6	133.1
15. Bicycles (d)	99	1071	1574	2042	2330	2677	3184
16. Sewing machines (d)	33	303	430	235	269	385	364

TABLE III-12 (Continued)

Industry (Unit)	1950-51	1960-61	1965-66	1970-71	1975-76	1976-77	1977-78
IV. Electrical Engineering Industries							
17. Power transformers (e)	0.18	4.11	4.46	8.09	13.9	15.1	15.6
18. Electric motors (f)	99	728	1753	2721	3610	3670	4040
19. Electric fans (g)	0.2	1.06	1.36	1.72	2.14	2.63	3.38
20. Electric lamps (g)	14.0	43.5	72.1	119.3	123.1	161.9	169.5
21. Radio receivers (d)	54	282	606	1794	1536	1685	1857
22. Electric cables and wires:							
(i) Aluminum conductors (b)	1.7	23.6	40.6	64.2	60.9	84.2	57.3
(ii) Bare copper conductors (b)	5	10.1	3.1	0.7	1.3	1.4	2.1
V. Chemicals and Allied Industries							
23. Nitrogenous fertilizers (j)	9	98	238	830	1535	1900	2013
24. Phosphatic fertilizers (k)	9	52	111	229	320	480	670
25. Sulphuric acid (b)	101	368	662	1053	1416	1902	2076
26. Soda ash (b)	45	152	331	449	555	568	572
27. Caustic soda (b)	12	101	218	371	467	506	52
28. Paper and paper board (b)	116	350	558	755	836	899	965
29. Rubber tires:							
(i) Auto tires (g)	0.87	1.44	2.31	3.79	5.40	6.25	6.17
(ii) Bicycle tires (g)	3.3	11.15	18.46	19.20	24.5	22.9	28.3
30. Cement (a)	2.73	7.97	10.82	14.40	17.2	18.8	19.3
31. Refractories (b)	237	567	695	683	729	788	790
32. Petroleum products refined (a)	0.2	5.8	9.4	17.1	21.0	21.6	23.2
VI. Textile Industries							
33. Jute textiles (b)	837	1097	1302	957	1302	1186	1178
34. Cotton yarn (h)	534	801	907	929	1105	1125	1128

35. Cotton cloth (i)	4215	6378	7440	7596	8348	8105	8141
(i) Mill sector (i)	3401	4649	4401	4055	4219	4161	4181
(ii) Decentralized sector (i)	814	2089	3039	3541	4129	3944	3960
36. Rayon yarn (b)	2.1	43.8	75.6	98.1	104.5	127.3	129.2
37. Artsilk fabrics (i)	287	544	878	947	875	1200	1350
38. Woollen manufactures:							
(i) Woollen and worsted yarn (h)	8.7	13.0	17.0	19.7	46.6	44.5	45.7
(ii) Woollen and worsted fabrics (i)	6.1	13.3	9.2	14.3	26.3	23.6	21.4
VII. Food Industries							
39. Sugar (Oct-Sep) (a)	1.13	3.03	3.51	3.74	4.64	4.84	6.45
40. Tea (h)	277	322	376	421	482	519	560
41. Coffee (b)	21	54.1	62.1	72.7	83.0	102.5	118.5
42. Vanaspati (b)	170	340	401	558	500	540	572
VIII. Electricity generated (e)	5300	16900	33000	55800	79850	89200	92180

(a) million tons   (d) thousands   (g) millions   (j) thousand tons of nitrogen
(b) thousand tons   (e) million kwh   (h) million kg   (k) thousand tons of phosphorous pentoxide
(c) million Rs.   (f) thousand-horsepower   (i) million meters

Source: *India: A Reference Annual, 1979*, pp. 301-302.

fertilizer and allied chemical plants. Bharat Heavy Electricals
Ltd. (BHEL), in Hyderabad, and Bharat Heavy Plates and Vessels Ltd. (BHPV) are the major public-sector organizations manufacturing equipment for the fertilizer industry.

Textiles. The textile industry is the largest industry in the
country. India is self-dependent on its local textile industry and
exports textiles and garments to several other countries. At the
end of 1977, there were 704 textile mills (412 spinning and 292
composite) with an installed capacity of 19.84 million spindles
and 208,000 looms. The production of cotton yarn in the organized sector in 1977 was 846 million kilograms and that of
cotton cloth was 3.2 billion meters. The decentralized sector of
handlooms and powerlooms produced another 3.67 billion meters
of cotton cloth.[30]

Cement. Manufacture of cement in India was first started in
Madras in 1904. At present, there are fifty-five cement factories,
ten of which are in the public sector, with a total installed capacity of 21.9 million tons per annum. Total production of cement in 1977-78 was 19.2 million tons as compared with 2.7
million tons in 1950-51.[31] Capacity is being increased in both
the private and the public sectors in order to meet India's growing demand for cement.

Drugs and Pharmaceuticals. Before 1947, most bulk drugs
were imported, and only processing and formulations were done
in India. Now, however, a larger percentage of bulk drugs is
being manufactured indigenously; in fact, drug manufacturing
has become a major industry. The value of drugs and pharmaceuticals produced during 1977-78 was about Rs. 9 billion compared to Rs. 120 million in 1948.[32] In an attempt to reduce the
dependence on bulk imports, the government has set up two
companies: Indian Drugs and Pharmaceuticals Ltd. and Hindustan Antibiotics Ltd. Three major objectives have been established that will govern the industry in the years to come.
The first objective is to double production in five years from the
1977-78 level of Rs. 8.5 billion to the sixth-plan target level of
Rs. 19 billion in 1982-83.[33] The second objective is to achieve

---

[30] *Ibid.,* p. 300.

[31] *Ibid.,* p. 305.

[32] *Ibid.,* p. 313.

[33] *India: A Reference Annual, 1977 & 78* (New Delhi: Publications
Division, Ministry of Information and Broadcasting, Government of India,
1978), p. 307.

self-sufficiency both in bulk drugs and in formulations. Third, multinational drug corporations, which have played a significant role in the development of the industry, are to be brought under the regulations of the government.

Automobile Industry. The automobile and commercial vehicle industry in India is not highly developed. The demand for and production of passenger cars is very small by Western standards, and heavy taxation and lack of incentives have prevented the industry from fully realizing its potential. Production of commercial vehicles, including jeeps, was 50,180 in 1977-78. Production of passenger cars in that year was 34,230, production of scooters was 159,030, and production of motorcycles was 68,360.

COMMERCE AND TRADE

Until 1947, India's trade was primarily agricultural and was confined to Britain and other commonwealth countries. Today, however, India has trading links with most countries in the world, and over 3,000 articles are on its export list.

In 1977-78, the total value of foreign trade (imports plus exports) was Rs. 114 billion, whereas in 1950-51, it was only 12.5 billion.[34] Table III-13 shows the growth of foreign trade and the balance of trade for the last thirty years.

TABLE III-13
Foreign Trade of India
(Billion Rs.)

Year	Imports	Exports (including re-exports)	Total Value of Foreign Trade	Balance of Trade
1950-51	6.5021	6.0064	12.5085	−.4957
1960-61	11.3969	6.6022	17.9991	−4.7947
1965-66	14.0853	8.0564	22.1417	−6.0289
1970-71	16.3420	15.3516	31.6936	−.9904
1973-74	29.5537	25.2340	54.7877	−4.3297
1974-75	45.1878	33.2883	78.4761	−11.8995
1975-76	52.6478	40.3626	93.0104	−12.2852
1976-77	50.7395	51.4578	102.1973	+.7183
1977-78	60.6860	53.7508	114.4368	−6.9352

Source: *India: A Reference Annual, 1979*, p. 329.

[34] *India: A Reference Annual, 1979*, p. 329.

Except for a few years in which there was a surplus, India's balance of trade has generally been in deficit. The deficit widened steadily between 1956 and 1966-67 because of the slow growth of exports. Subsequently, however, the deficit declined as a result of slower growth of imports. The decline lasted until 1970-71; then in 1971-72, the deficit again widened. In 1972-73, however, because of an appreciable increase in exports, the balance of trade was favorable for the first time in twenty-five years. From 1972-73 to 1975-76, the deficit again grew steadily; there was a net surplus in 1976-77, but a deficit occurred again in 1977-78.

India's overall exports during the first half of 1977-78 amounted to Rs. 25.85 billion and total imports were Rs. 24.15 billion, resulting in a surplus of commodities. Tea, cotton textiles, iron ore and concentrates, tobacco, jute, engineering goods, and handicrafts are among the main exports of India. Table III-14 gives the principal exports by commodities and the trend over the last several years.

Imports increased over the years until 1967-68, when a decline began that continued until 1969-70. The decline was primarily due to reduced food grain imports, indigenous substitution, and slack in domestic demand. There was a sharp increase in imports during 1974-75 and 1975-76, because imports of free food and fertilizers were larger. In 1976-77, imports declined to 50.74 billion from Rs. 52.65 billion in the earlier year. Table III-15 shows principal imports and the trend in their growth over the years.

The United States has been the largest supplier of imports, mainly as a result of imports of foodgrains and other items under aid and grants. Iran was the second largest supplier primarily because of oil imports. An appreciable increase also occurred during the last five years in imports from the U.S.S.R., Japan, Belgium, West Germany, Italy, and Saudi Arabia. Table III-16 indicates import volumes from India's principal trading partners. The United Kingdom and the United States were India's principal buyers until 1968-69. Since then, Japan and the U.S.S.R. have also become principal buyers. Other important buyers are France, West Germany, Italy, the Netherlands, Bangladesh, Singapore, Poland, Switzerland, Iraq, Indonesia, and Iran. Table III-17 shows countrywide exports for the last several years.

TABLE III-14
Exports of Principal Commodities
(millions Rs.)

	1950-51	1965-66	1970-71	1973-74	1974-75	1975-76	1976-77
Tea	798.9	1148.4	1482.5	1460.3	2280.6	2369.1	2931.4
Coffee	13.5	129.4	251.1	460.1	513.6	666.5	1148.5
Tobacco (unmanufactured)	141.1	195.7	314.0	684.1	803.6	931.3	966.2
Jute (manufactured inclu. twist and yarn)	1127.7	1891.7	1891.7	2257.3	2940.3	2508.3	2008.3
Oilcakes	.3	346.4	554.2	1781.9	959.6	861.2	2238.1
Cashew kernels	85.5	274.0	5.206	744.3	1181.6	961.3	105.9
Sugar	1.7	111.9	293.0	425.9	3393.3	4723.3	1481.2
Vegetable oils (nonessentials)	252.6	40.9	70.3	316.5	336.6	352.6	485.8
Leather & leather manfrs.	257.7	282.1	715.9	1665.7	1338.8	2014.8	2634.9
Cotton piecegoods	1179.7	552.4	752.9	1950.4	1589.5	1587.4	2539.6
a) Mill-made	1071.7	469.1	675.0	1626.6	1296.5	1193.9	2007.9
b) Handloom	108.0	83.3	77.9	323.8	292.6	393.5	531.7
Cotton Apparel	11.5	63.6	302.0	674.0	969.2	1449.1	2570.0
Pearls, precious & semi-precious stones, worked, unworked	N.A.	232.6	418.8	1069.0	984.0	1229.4	2424.3
Chemicals & allied products (excl. essential oils and plastic materials)	N.A.	91.4	293.6	503.0	929.1	844.5	1091.0
Silver	—	Negl.	Negl.	56.4	818.4	1878.5	1514.3
Fish & fish preparations	24.6	65.9	305.4	892.4	661.7	1265.6	1802.5

TABLE III-14 (Continued)

	1950-51	1965-66	1970-71	1973-74	1974-75	1975-76	1976-77
Iron ore and concentrates	2.2	423.7	1172.8	1328.7	1603.9	2139.3	2384.9
Woolen carpets, carpeting, floor rugs & materials	55.6	44.8	99.6	240.6	336.5	454.6	452.3
Iron and steel	28.7	123.8	672.0	261.8	210.6	680.1	2829.9
Engineering goods	N.S.S.	198.0	1304.1	2016.8	3565.7	4129.7	5544.3
TOTAL (including other items)	6006.4	8056.4	15351.6	25234.0	33288.3	40428.1	51457.8

N.S.S.   Not separately specified.
N.A.   Not available.
Source: *India: A Reference Annual, 1979*, p. 331.

TABLE III-15
Imports of Principal Commodities
(million Rs.)

	1950-51	1965-66	1970-71	1972-73	1973-74	1974-75	1975-76	1976-77
Milk and cream (dried or condensed)	35.6	66.4	70.4	179.4	149.9	182.5	203.6	309.9
Vegetable oils	33.4	71.1	230.8	155.0	569.4	123.0	141.9	1006.1
Oil seeds, nuts & kernels	22.9	88.1	63.6	123.2	73.7	100.7	78.5	33.0
Fresh fruits and nuts	95.1	188.6	358.2	406.8	364.0	471.7	420.2	284.9
Wheat, unmilked	992.1	2647.3	1733.7	481.6	3461.0	6981.8	12105.5	8071.0
Rice	534.9	419.0	298.2	107.1	64.5	121.7	465.8	459.8
Raw cotton	1000.7	462.1	988.3	908.8	520.5	266.7	282.2	1294.6
Raw jute	.7	91.6	1.4	11.3	122.2	37.5	33.3	67.6
Iron & steel	143.1	980.0	1470.4	2258.1	2494.6	4172.8	3119.0	2197.3
Raw wool & hair	56.2	51.2	160.7	118.8	209.5	274.8	259.2	279.8
Machinery (electric & nonelectric)	914.2	4216.0	3281.6	4319.5	5566.2	5644.8	7774.5	8317.4
Transport equipment	349.3	705.5	665.5	1001.2	949.7	1312.2	1571.3	1474.0
Manufactures of metals	139.4	181.7	92.8	187.9	218.9	276.2	331.4	287.2
Copper	84.9	333.7	602.0	519.0	708.3	730.2	218.4	461.6
Zinc	65.6	128.4	219.7	228.6	277.2	553.6	213.1	356.0
Aluminum	23.8	32.9	33.5	28.7	28.7	30.5	99.5	23.1
Petroleum (crude & partly refined)	N.A.	348.7	1059.0	1448.2	4170.9	95.490	10528.0	11516.2

TABLE III-15 (Continued)

	1950-51	1965-66	1970-71	1972-73	1973-74	1974-75	1975-76	1976-77
Chemical elements & compounds	91.7	358.6	679.8	913.8	1096.6	1788.2	1802.0	1372.5
Medicinal & pharmaceutical products	99.7	87.3	242.7	232.2	264.3	340.6	362.6	421.4
Fertilizers manufactured	123.5	389.0	612.0	962.6	1628.4	4362.0	4694.1	1977.2
Newsprint	53.7	61.8	187.3	205.2	184.8	449.9	383.2	472.0
Synthetic & regenerated fibre (man-made fibre)	N.A.	N.A.	72.1	49.4	25.4	27.2	63.4	301.5
TOTAL (including other items)	6502.1	14085.3	16342.0	18674.4	29553.7	45199.3	52652.0	50151.5 50739.5 (R)

N.A.   Not Available.
Source: *India: A Reference Annual, 1979*, p. 334.

TABLE III-16
Imports from Principal Countries
(millions Rs.)

Country	1950-51	1965-66	1970-71	1971-72	1973-74	1974-75	1975-76	1976-77
Australia	334.5	241.8	365.8	1338.5	438.1	1184.8	1016.7	2536.0
Bangladesh	—	—	—	34.6	170.4	91.8	46.5	60.7
Belgium	92.2	115.1	115.1	510.4	657.1	1019.0	864.9	575.0
Burma	188.0	97.2	96.4	20.5	.7	.1	26.3	5.5
Canada	219.0	315.4	1172.3	1076.1	1158.6	1304.2	2320.1	1294.0
Czechoslovakia	27.7	211.5	202.0	159.1	267.1	333.1	530.1	341.3
Egypt	328.7	199.5	398.4	288.7	269.0	228.3	189.9	211.5
France	110.7	180.5	213.4	393.5	702.9	811.6	1965.3	1411.0
Germany (West)	—	1371.4	1074.7	1725.8	2057.9	3068.7	3699.6	3070.0
Iran	370.0	340.8	916.4	121.98	2675.8	4726.6	4598.8	5078.7
Italy	162.6	198.6	288.6	359.4	494.0	783.8	848.3	574.4
Japan	101.1	793.3	834.3	1785.3	2595.3	4534.7	3611.8	2970.5
Kenya	185.2	45.6	96.9	63.2	174.3	98.3	87.7	70.0
Malaysia	8.1	127.7	57.5	84.2	320.9	112.0	145.8	339.8
Netherlands	72.6	197.7	190.9	366.9	565.6	475.9	638.3	657.0
Saudi Arabia	8.7	86.6	241.7	448.4	1313.5	2976.5	2901.3	3319.8
Singapore	160.8	—	11.7	28.3	97.2	72.2	116.6	87.9
Sudan	74.9	57.4	209.4	458.0	219.3	50.3	36.4	190.4
Sweden	52.9	106.3	98.0	189.3	239.3	259.9	684.7	357.5
Switzerland	76.1	145.1	115.7	116.5	169.5	365.2	554.1	90.4
UK	1353.1	1500.9	1267.6	2372.5	2521.7	2134.0	2840.0	3295.0
USA	1191.6	5348.3	4529.5	2348.7	4984.3	7290.9	12852.2	10593.0
USSR	2.3	831.7	1061.3	1143.7	2547.3	4024.9	3097.8	3320.0
TOTAL (including other countries)	6502.1	14085.3	16342.0	18674.4	29553.7	45199.3	52652.0	50737.9

Source: *India: A Reference Annual, 1979*, p. 335.

TABLE III-17

Exports to Principal Countries

(*millions Rs.*)

Country	1950-51	1965-66	1970-71	1972-73	1973-74	1974-75	1975-76	1976-77
Argentina	106.5	41.5	33.4	7.7	64.2	106.3	39.8	22.9
Australia	297.1	174.9	344.6	259.8	507.8	614.1	482.1	651.8
Bangladesh	—	—	—	1682.4	587.8	422.0	621.9	545.7
Burma	244.6	35.7	140.3	43.6	15.4	46.5	92.8	90.4
Canada	137.9	202.7	279.6	282.0	310.9	441.8	458.0	498.8
Cuba	—	2.9	1.6	.1	—	—	—	—
Czechoslovakia	100.8	159.3	294.6	461.0	437.9	603.8	347.1	447.0
Egypt	58.7	270.5	563.7	317.2	148.8	525.8	1001.3	908.9
France	91.0	110.3	179.8	459.0	497.0	862.2	862.2	1770.3
Germany (West)	—	179.7	323.1	622.8	167.9	1061.7	1179.1	2297.7
Indonesia	4.2	8.2	41.0	53.0	267.8	509.6	517.2	605.8
Italy	150.0	93.9	140.1	488.5	693.5	524.3	800.2	1190.0
Japan	102.7	570.5	2034.8	2171.6	3587.5	2966.5	4327.6	5441.5
Kenya	64.1	48.6	78.7	55.0	102.8	154.0	157.2	199.4
Malaysia	55.0	125.9	117.3	93.4	246.3	292.6	328.5	299.0
Netherlands	101.6	79.1	139.8	354.0	733.4	717.5	822.3	1952.9
New Zealand	36.7	65.7	59.7	82.5	135.5	207.4	129.0	135.0
Nigeria	46.2	40.0	86.2	96.5	114.9	216.1	375.5	249.9
Singapore	306.8	—	176.3	178.4	435.4	367.9	530.5	588.3
Sri Lanka	196.8	127.9	318.2	80.1	98.4	268.5	231.1	393.5
Sudan	41.8	81.7	382.7	207.1	185.9	664.6	365.2	525.0
UK	1398.2	1447.8	1704.4	1725.3	2631.4	3122.6	4213.2	5206.9
USA	1158.8	1469.8	2073.4	2757.4	3459.2	3749.3	5199.8	5759.7
USSR	13.8	928.9	2098.5	3048.2	2860.2	4213.5	4166.9	4459.0
TOTAL (including other countries)	6006.4	8056.4	15351.6	19708.3	25234.0	33288.3	40428.1	51432.3

Source: *India: A Reference Annual, 1979*, p. 337.

EMPLOYMENT AND WAGES

The 1971 census report indicated that the working population of India was about 180.5 million (32.92 percent of the total population). Of this working population, only 10 percent worked in industries, government, commerce, and services (organized sector); the rest of the working population was employed in agriculture, retailing, and small domestic industries, (unorganized sector). Cultivators and laborers formed the bulk of the unorganized sector—43.38 percent and 26.32 percent respectively. Table III-18 gives the distribution of working population according to activity and sex. Most labor legislation and programs are limited to the organized sector. The largest number of workers in this sector is employed in factories. In 1974, the estimated average daily employment stood at 5.68 million. Total employment in the organized sector in 1976 was 20.21 million compared with only 12.09 million in 1961. A large percentage of this employment is in the public sector for which the percentage of total employed increased from 58.3 percent to 66.1 percent in the same period. Table III-19 shows the overall employment in the organized sector for the years 1961 to 1976. In 1976, the major employers were in the services industry, manufacturing, transport and communications, and the agricultural sector. Distribution of employment in the organized sector is given by industry in Table III-20.

Unemployment in India has grown steadily in absolute as well as proportionate terms. Total unemployment in 1971 has been estimated at 9 million, with 7.7 million unemployed in rural areas and 1.3 million in urban areas.[35] As one measure for reducing unemployment, in 1945 the government instituted the National Employment Service, which consisted of a network of employment exchanges. In 1977, there were 594 exchanges nationwide. The list of unemployed registered with the employment exchanges grew from 758,503 in 1956 to over 10.9 million in 1977.[36] This increase in unemployment was caused primarily by population increases, migration from rural to urban areas, and the slow growth of the industrial sector. The government has been attempting to reduce the problem by giving priority to employment-generating projects.

---

[35] *Quarterly Economic Review of India, Nepal,* Annual Supplement, 1979, p. 7.

[36] *India: A Reference Annual, 1979,* p. 386.

TABLE III-18
Distribution of Working Population (1971 Census)
(millions)

Category	Male		Female		Total	
	Number	Percentage share in total male population	Number	Percentage share in total female population	Number	Percentage share in total population
Total Population	284.1	100.00	264.1	100.00	548.2	100.00
A. Total Working Population	149.2	52.51	31.3	11.86	180.5	32.92
(i) Cultivators	69.0	24.28	9.3	3.52	78.3	14.28
(ii) Agricultural laborers	31.7	11.16	15.8	5.98	47.5	8.66
(iii) Livestock, forestry, fishing, hunting and plantations, orchards and allied activities	3.5	1.24	.8	0.30	4.3	0.78
(iv) Mining and quarrying	.8	0.28	.1	0.05	.9	0.17
(v) (a) Household industry	5.0	1.77	1.3	0.50	6.3	1.16
(b) Other than household industry	9.9	3.47	.9	0.33	10.8	1.96
(vi) Construction	2.0	0.71	.2	0.08	2.2	0.40
(vii) Trade and commerce	9.5	3.34	.6	0.21	10.1	1.83
(viii) Transport, storage and communications	4.3	1.50	.1	0.05	4.4	0.80
(ix) Other services	13.5	4.76	2.2	0.84	15.7	2.88
B. Non-working population	134.9	47.49	232.8	88.14	367.7	67.08

Source: *India: A Reference Annual 1979*, p. 373.

TABLE III-19

Overall Employment in Organized Sector

End of March	Public Sector				Private sector	Grand total
	Central Govt.	State Govts.	Quasi-Govt.	Total *		
Employment (Mn.)						
1961	2.09	3.01	0.77	7.06	5.04	12.09
1966	2.64	3.72	1.32	9.38	6.81	16.19
1972	2.85	4.36	2.18	11.31	6.77	18.08
1973	2.92	4.58	2.58	11.98	6.85	18.82
1974	2.94	4.71	2.91	12.49	6.79	19.28
1975	2.99	4.77	3.19	12.89	6.80	19.69
1976	3.05	4.94	3.39	13.36	6.84	20.21†
Share in employment (%)						
1961	17.3	24.9	6.4	58.3	41.7	100.0
1966	16.3	23.0	8.1	57.9	42.1	100.0
1972	15.8	24.1	12.0	62.5	37.4	100.0
1973	15.5	24.3	13.7	63.6	36.4	100.0
1974	15.2	24.4	15.1	64.9	35.3	100.0
1975	15.2	24.2	16.2	65.5	34.5	100.0
1976	15.1	24.4	16.8	66.1	33.9	100.0
Annual growth (%)						
1966	2.6	3.8	9.3	4.7	12.7	7.9
1972	3.0	4.9	12.8	5.3	0.4	3.4
1973	2.2	5.1	18.5	5.9	1.2	4.1
1974	0.7	2.8	13.0	4.3	−0.8	2.4
1975	1.7	1.3	9.6	3.2	0.1	2.1
1976	1.9	3.6	6.3	3.7	0.7	2.6

Note: Data in this Table and the next cover all establishments in public sector and all nonagricultural establishments in private sector employing 25 or more persons. Private establishments employing 10 to 24 workers are also covered on a voluntary basis.

  * Including Local Bodies.

  † In Dec. 1976, 20.40 mn., of which 13.62 mn. in public sector and 6.78 mn. in private sector.

Source: *Statistical Outline of India: 1978*, p. 120.

Industrial training institutes have been set up all over the country to impart skills in thirty-one engineering and twenty-one nonengineering trades to young men and women between the ages of fifteen and twenty-five. At present, 429 such institutes are providing free training facilities to about 157,000 crafts-men.[37] This, combined with other training institutions in both

---

[37] *India: A Reference Annual, 1979*, p. 388.

TABLE III-20
Employment in Organized Sector by Industry Division

End of March:	1961	1966	1975	1976
		'000s		
Public sector	7,050	9,379	12,899	13,363
Agriculture, hunting *etc.*	180	227	340	401
Mining & quarrying	129	160	694	719
Manufacturing	369	670	1,019	1,113
Construction	603	766	955	992
Electricity, gas & water	224	303	509	536
Wholesale & retail trade *etc.*	94	155	53	56
Transport & communication	1,724	2,094	2,364	2,418
Services *	3,727	5,004	6,956	7,129
Private sector	5,040	6,813	6,799	6,844
Agriculture, hunting *etc.*	670	903	818	827
Mining & quarrying	550	507	123	132
Manufacturing	3,020	3,858	4,102	4,158
Construction	240	254	127	94
Electricity, gas & water	40	42	39	35
Wholesale & retail trade *etc.*	160	330	309	287
Transport & communication	80	123	79	74
Services *	280	796	1,201	1,238
Total employment	12,090	16,192	19,688	20,207
Agriculture, hunting *etc.*	850	1,130	1,158	1,228
Mining & quarrying	679	667	817	851
Manufacturing	3,389	4,528	5,121	5,271
Construction	843	1,020	1,082	1,086
Electricity, gas & water	264	345	548	571
Wholesale & retail trade *etc.*	254	485	362	343
Transport & communication	1,804	2,217	2,443	2,492
Services *	4,007	5,800	8,157	8,367

Note: See Note to Table III-19.
   * Includes financing, insurance, real estate, community, social & personal
   services.
Source: *Statistical Outline of India: 1978*, p. 121.

the public and the private sectors, is generating a large work
force of skilled technicians and workers, and new industries
normally do not face major problems in recruiting skilled labor.
   The Indian worker earns one of the lowest wages anywhere
in the world. The low labor costs would make India a very attractive location for labor-intensive industries were it not for
the complex maze of government regulation. The per capita

earnings of factory workers in 1974 were Rs. 3,131 (approximately $410) with the highest wages, of Rs. 3,988, in the jute and textiles industries (see Table III-21). The payment of wages is governed by the Payment of Wages Act, 1936, and the Minimum Wages Act, 1948, as amended subsequently. These acts are discussed in greater detail in Chapter V.

Wages and employment are two major issues facing both workers and employers today. The industry has aimed to keep wages down in order to increase the competitiveness of their products in international and domestic markets. Costs of the products are high in the first place due to lack of economies of

TABLE III-21

Per Capita Annual Earnings of Factory Workers
(Industry-wise)

	1971	1972 *	1973 *	1974 *
		Rupees		
Cotton textiles	2,799	3,000	3,237	3,170
Wool, silk & synthetic textiles	2,899	3,090	3,224	3,388
Jute textiles *etc.*	2,776	3,338	3,629	3,988
Textile products	2,485	2,792	2,887	3,095
Wood & products	1,849	2,062	2,114	2,247
Paper & products & printing, publishing *etc.*	2,873	2,956	3,218	3,232
Leather & products	2,852	2,871	2,841	2,778
Rubber, plastic, petroleum & coal products	2,554	2,757	2,736	2,641
Chemicals & products	2,899	2,996	3,015	3,204
Non-metallic mineral products	1,880	2,005	2,250	2,195
Basic metal & alloys	3,165	3,218	3,165	2,994
Metal products	2,575	2,527	2,740	2,815
Electrical machinery *etc.*	3,076	3,276	3,274	3,239
Other machinery	2,795	3,057	3,036	3,066
Transport equipment	3,496	3,731	3,616	3,180
Electricity	3,441	3,558	3,573	3,639
All industries (incl. others) †	2,821	3,008	3,136	3,131

Note: Figures relate to employees receiving wage/salary of less than Rs. 400 per month. Earnings include basic wage, dearness allowance, overtime, other cash allowances, annual profit bonus and money value of concessions.

  * Provisional.

  † Excluding Railway workshops and seasonal industries like food.

Source: *Statistical Outline of India: 1978*, p. 124.

scale. Workers and unions have, on the other hand, strived to keep wages in line with the almost constant inflation, which has reached all time highs in the last years.

FOREIGN INVESTMENT

India's post-independence policy toward foreign investment has been to welcome it on a very selective basis, restricting it to fields in which the government feels it will be advantageous to the economy. Political ideology and the fact that over the past thirty years India has achieved a diversified industrial base have changed the fields in which such investment is sought and encouraged. In spite of the government's evident anti-foreign investment stand, which is prompted more by political than by economic reasons, foreign investment has continued to play a significant role in Indian industry, especially in industries such as drugs, pharmaceuticals, and chemicals. Foreign investment in the form of capital participation and joint ventures is still welcomed in high technology, employment-generating, and export-oriented projects.

The total foreign investment in 1974 was Rs. 19.43 billion, up from Rs. 8.94 billion in 1964. The largest share of this investment was in manufacturing (see Table III-22). The United Kingdom had the largest investment outstanding in 1974 at Rs. 6.891 billion, followed closely by the United States with Rs. 5.309 billion.

Foreign investment in India is governed under the industrial policy, and the Ministry of Industry directs and regulates foreign investment and collaboration and has specified the industries in which foreign investment can be made and the form in which such an investment shall be allowed. The government earlier had listed three categories which comprised: (1) industries in which foreign investment is permitted with or without technical collaboration; (2) industries in which foreign technical collaboration may be permitted, but not foreign investment; and (3) industries in which no foreign collaboration (either financial or technical) was considered necessary. In December 1978, the government replaced these three categories with a list of industries in which no collaboration, either financial or technical, is considered necessary (see Appendix C). The ban on investment in these industries is to be applied in a flexible manner in order to allow foreign collaboration on merit. The ban applied to twenty-two broad industries covering over 200 products.

TABLE III-22
Foreign Business Investment Outstanding
(million Rs.)

	End March 1964	1974
Total	8,940	19,430
By industry		
Plantations	1,090	1,136
Mining	137	169
Petroleum	1,674	1,758
Manufacturing	4,364	10,732
of which:		
foods, beverages, etc.	348	647
metals & metal products	997	1,535
chemicals & allied products	856	4,105
Services	1,875	5,635
By type		
Direct investments	5,655	9,134
of which:		
branches	2,597	2,416
subsidiaries	2,399	4,704
other control	659	2,014
Other capital		
of which:		
equity holdings by non-residents	530	1,077
private & official creditor capital (net liabilities)	2,755	8,761
By source		
UK	5,084	6,891
USA	1,660	5,309
West Germany	239	1,808
Italy	114	834
Japan	301	416
Switzerland	187	449
France	205	497
International institutions	724	1,212

Source: *Quarterly Economic Review of India, Nepal*, Annual Supplement, 1979.

Despite the political rhetoric, some of the restrictions on foreign investment were eased in 1978. The government of Morarji Desai sought to curb the influence of India's big business houses and this resulted in a more flexible attitude toward foreign collaboration and investment. In 1978, the number of investment and licensing approvals rose to 307 (see Table III-23), and the amount of approved investment doubled from Rs. 40 million to Rs. 94 million. Industrial machinery and electrical equipment continued to be the preferred areas for foreign investors, and equity participations, though still insignificant, continued to increase in importance.[38]

The United States, the second largest investor in India, had a total investment of $328 million in 1978, which had decreased slightly from $337 million in 1977.[39] A major reason for this decline was the dilution of foreign firm equity holdings in Indian companies under the Foreign Exchange Regulation Act (FERA). FERA requires that foreign firms gradually reduce their equity holding to 40 percent. A number of multinationals, however, decided to pull out of the country, notable among these companies being Coca-Cola, IBM, Remington Rand, and Kaiser Aluminum.[40] A large number of firms have reduced their equity ownership and are continuing to maintain a significant presence in the country.

The profitability and sales of foreign firms in India have shown modest improvements in the last five years. In fiscal year 1977-78, profits of most of thirty-three leading foreign firms in India increased. Profits of firms in the rubber and tire, aluminum, and nonelectrical machinery industries did not increase.[41] In 1978, the rate of return on U.S. direct investment in India increased significantly from 3 percent in 1977 to 11.6 percent in 1978.[42]

Since the change in government in 1980, Mrs. Gandhi has continued to encourage foreign investment, though on a moderate scale, especially in the area of oil technology.

---

[38] "India: Investment and Licensing Grow," *Business Asia*, Vol. XI, No. 44 (November 2, 1979), p. 351.

[39] "Important Reversal in U.S. Investment in Asia/Pacific Region," *Business Asia*, Vol. XI, No. 51 (December 21, 1979), p. 404.

[40] "Prospects for Profits: India, the Next Five Years," *Business International*, Vol. XXVI, No. 48 (November 30, 1979), p. 383.

[41] "Profitability in India Rose for Foreign Firms During Fiscal 1977-1978," *Business Asia*, Vol. XI, No. 25 (June 22, 1979), pp. 197-198.

[42] "U.S. Profitability in Asia: Europe and Latin America Outpaced Ninth Time," *Business Asia*, Vol. XI, No. 43 (October 26, 1979), p. 341.

TABLE III-23

Foreign Investment Trends 1973-78

	1973	1974	1975	1976	1977	1978
Number of projects approved	265	359	271	277	267	307
(Total direct investment projects)	(34)	(55)	(40)	(39)	(27)	(44)
Country of origin:						
— UK	53(5)	59(7)	54(3)	55(3)	59(9)	61(5)
— US	48(12)	79(17)	55(13)	69(17)	54(6)	59(16)
— Germany	60(7)	71(10)	59(11)	58(8)	55(5)	58(8)
— Japan	38(3)	28(4)	23(3)	10(—)	20(—)	28(3)
— France	13(1)	22(5)	13(2)	17(2)	14(1)	21(—)
— Others	53(6)	100(12)	67(8)	69(9)	65(6)	80(12)
Preferred investment areas:						
— Industrial machinery	54	69	50	57	74	76
— Electrical equipment	55	72	53	63	67	46
— Chemicals (other than fertilizer)	16	41	40	32	23	30
— Transportation	31	34	15	18	18	20
— Machine tools	19	14	12	19	10	20
— Mining	11	23	19	12	7	18
— Others	79	106	82	76	68	67

Source: *Business Asia*, November 2, 1979, p. 351.

CHAPTER IV

Organized Labor in India

The organization of labor in India followed closely upon the industrial development of the country, which started in the latter half of the nineteenth century. The earliest labor activities took place in the textile mills of Bombay and Ahmedabad. The first official strike was declared in 1895 [1] by weavers in Ahmedabad who were protesting the substitution of a fortnightly wage system for a weekly system by the Ahmedabad Mill Owners Association. Other strikes took place sporadically throughout the first quarter of the twentieth century in industrial towns such as Calcutta, Madras, and Bombay.

N. M. Lokhande, a factory worker from Bombay, may be said to be the founder of the organized labor movement in India. In 1884, he organized a demonstration at which requests were presented to the newly appointed Factory Commission. In 1890, he convened a mass meeting of dissatisfied mill workers and was able to obtain some benefits from the mill owners of Bombay. Subsequently, he organized the Bombay Mill Hands Association, and started *Dinabandhu* (Friend of the Poor), the first working class newspaper.[2]

Even though the seeds of trade unionism were planted in the late nineteenth century, it was not until the time of the First World War that trade union activity became an organized movement in India. The growing movement for independence from British colonial rule had a major impact on the development of the labor movement.

The Madras Labour Union, formed in 1918, was the first group to be formed along the lines of a modern trade union. Its members were textile workers employed in the Buckingham and

---

[1] G. Ramanujam, *The Story of Indian Labour* (New Delhi: Indian National Trade Union Congress, 1967), pp. 6-7.

[2] V. V. Giri, *Labour Problems in Indian Industry* (Bombay: Asia Publishing House, 1958), p. 2.

Carnatic Mills, and the organization was started by B. P. Wadia, a leader in the national independence movement. Around the same time, Ansuyabhen Sarabhai organized textile workers in Ahmedabad, leading to the 1918 strike led by Mahatma Gandhi and to the foundation of the Textile Labour Association in 1920.[3]

These developments catalyzed the formation of trade unions in various industrial centers of the country. It is true that economic conditions were the major cause of trade union activities in the country, but it is important to understand the boost given to trade unionism by the upsurge in the national independence movement. Because Indian industries were owned predominantly by Europeans, the distinction between the two movements became increasingly difficult to establish, and trade unions in India today remain strongly tied to the political parties.

DEVELOPMENT OF THE TRADE UNION MOVEMENT

The growth of the trade union movement in India can be divided into four periods during which distinct changes in the nature of the movement were witnessed.

The Post-World War I Period—1919-1930

Soon after World War I, in 1919, a labor wing of the League of Nations was formed and called the International Labor Organization (ILO). India was a founding member of the ILO and Indian labor representatives attended the first ILO conference in Washington in 1919. It was realized then that a central organization for the Indian trade union movement would facilitate the selection of Indian representatives to the ILO and help in the coordination and organization of the Indian movement. This realization led to the establishment in 1920 of the All-India Trade Union Congress (AITUC), which claimed sixty-four affiliated unions with a total membership of 140,854 workers. Of this number, 91,427 represented the railroad industry, 19,800 were from the shipping industry, and the rest represented other industries. A number of unions, the most prominent among them being the Textile Labour Association of Ahmedabad, remained unaffiliated.[4]

---

[3] V. B. Karnik, *Indian Trade Unions: A Survey* (Bombay, Popular Prakashan, 1978), pp. 24-27.

[4] Ramanujam, *The Story of Indian Labour*, p. 13.

The AITUC, from its inception, followed the Trades Union Congress of the United Kingdom in philosophy and practice. The AITUC concerned itself with the overall political and economic welfare of its members, but was ineffective in advising the local unions on how to handle their grievances and organize their activities. The ideological leadership of the Indian trade union movement was provided, until 1925, by the more liberal leaders of the Indian National Congress (INC). Although the strong influence in the AITUC of the leaders of the INC, the only major political party at the time, gave the AITUC a strong political character, it also rendered it less of a labor organization, for the political activities of the AITUC officers prevented them from providing undivided attention to the trade union activity. This was further demonstrated by the election of the president of the INC, Lala Lajpat Rai, as the first president of the AITUC.[5]

In the second half of the 1920s, however, the local Communists, aided by Soviet Russia and the Communist Party of Great Britain, consolidated their hold on the AITUC and openly proposed its disaffiliation from the INC. During the tenth session of the AITUC, held at Nagpur in December 1929, the Communists prevailed and voted to dissociate the AITUC from the INC and the ILO, and to affiliate it with international communist organizations. This forced the nationalists out of the AITUC, and this group then formed the Indian Trade Union Federation (ITUF).[6] The AITUC continues its strong communist character to this day.

Strike activity during the 1920s was widespread, stimulated partly by the newly found power of the trade unions and partly by the postwar recession which led to layoffs and reductions in wages. Faced with economic uncertainty and rising prices, workers found strikes the only way to express their discontent, and during 1921, 396 strikes were reported, involving some 600,351 workers and accounting for a loss of about 7 million workdays.[7] The upsurge of strike activity after 1918 was the most intense and widespread strike movement in India to that date.

The onset of depression in Indian industry in 1922-23 severely hit the textile industry, which was the major organized industry

---

[5] *Ibid.*, p. 14.

[6] *Ibid.*, p. 22.

[7] Karnik, *Indian Trade Unions*, p. 409.

at that time. Employers in Bombay and Ahmedabad attempted to reduce labor costs by announcing wage cuts and reductions in annual bonuses. A large number of strikes took place to protest these moves. In 1923, 43,000 workers from 56 mills were on strike in Ahmedabad for over two months, causing the loss of nearly 2,400,000 man-days.

The Bombay Millowners Association announced in 1923 that bonus payments would be suspended because of bad economic conditions. This resulted in a general strike which started on January 17, 1924, involved over 160,000 workers, and accounted for a loss of 7,750,000 man-days of work. The long strike was, however, partly successful, preventing a wage cut at the Bombay textile mill.

During this period, the Indian trade union movement received its first contribution from an international trade union with the contribution of £ 1,250 by the British Trade Union Congress for the strike fund of the Bombay textile workers.[8] Indian strike activity thus received widespread acceptance in trade union circles during this period. Table IV-1 contains data on industrial disputes in India from 1921 to 1926.

TABLE IV-1
Industrial Disputes in India—1921-1926

	No. of Strikes and Lockouts	No. of Workers Involved	No. of Working Days Lost
1921	396	600,351	6,984,426
1922	278	435,434	3,972,727
1923	213	301,044	5,051,794
1924	133	312,462	8,730,918
1925	134	270,423	12,578,129
1926	128	186,811	1,097,478

Source: V. B. Karnik, *Indian Trade Unions: A Survey* (Bombay: Popular Prakashan, 1978), p. 409.

The most significant development during this phase of Indian trade union history was, however, the passage of a legislative act, the Indian Trade Unions Act, by the government of India in 1926. This act gave legal status to registered trade unions, thus conferring on them and their members a measure of immunity from civil suits and criminal prosecution. This enhanced

---

[8] Chamanlal Revri, *The Indian Trade Union Movement—An Outline History 1880-1947* (New Delhi: Orient Longman, 1972), pp. 99-103.

their acceptance by the government, and the resultant publicity given to trade unions gave the movement a strong momentum. Even though a lot of unions remained unregistered, the major organizations were represented by registered unions. The number of trade unions registered under the act in 1929 was eighty-seven with a total membership of 183,000.[9]

The Pre-World War II Period—1930-1939

The period from 1930 to 1935 was one of the worst for the Indian trade union movement. The worldwide depression of the early 1930s had a major impact on the Indian worker and on the trade union movement. Beset, furthermore, by organizational weaknesses, political differences, and fragmentation of the central unions, the movement suffered a severe setback, showing a marked recession of the progress made during the 1920s. Although the period from 1935 to 1939 saw a recovery of momentum in trade union activity, the divisiveness that afflicted the movement between 1929 and 1934 has remained manifest in the nature of the trade unions ever since.

A further split occurred in the Communist-controlled AITUC after the 1931 session in Calcutta when the extreme Communist group, led by S. V. Deshpande, left the AITUC and formed the All-India Red Trade Union Congress. Thus, the Indian labor movement was being fragmented at a time when it needed all its unity and strength to fight the depression and the threat of retrenchment and wage cuts.

The ITUF, which had been formed by the dissident nationalists who left the AITUC in 1929, and the Railway Trade Unions, which were not part of the AITUC, met in Calcutta in April 1933 and formed the National Trade Union Federation (NTUF). Forty-seven unions were affiliated at the time with a membership of 145,000.[10]

It was realized later, however, that fragmented, the trade union movement was ineffectual in protecting the interests of the working class. From this realization and from the unhappy experiences of failed strikes, arose the determination to strive for unity in the movement.

In 1935, the All-India Red Trade Union Congress, led by the extreme Communists, merged with the AITUC. This merger

[9] Giri, *Labour Problems in Indian Industry*, p. 12.

[10] Ramanujam, *The Story of Indian Labour*, p. 39.

was brought about by attrition in the ranks of the All-India Red Trade Union Congress as well as by ideological and tactical guidance from Moscow. Efforts to reunite the NTUF and the AITUC began soon after the Bombay session of the AITUC, held in 1936. The political climate was generally in favor of unity in the ranks of labor at that time, the purpose being to strengthen the movement. In 1938, the Unity Conference was held in Nagpur and the AITUC accepted the merger terms suggested by the NTUF. One of the major conditions of the agreement was that no political decision should be taken, unless approved by a two-thirds majority. Unity was finally achieved in 1940, with N. M. Joshi becoming the general secretary of the united AITUC.

The worldwide depression of the early 1930s had a major impact on the Indian worker and the Indian trade union movement. In 1933, more than 50,000 workers in Bombay alone were thrown out of their jobs.[11] Most employers, faced with a major downturn in demand for their business, introduced wage cuts, and a fragmented trade union movement resorted to strikes that failed totally to achieve any purpose. In 1934, the Communists launched a general strike in the textile industry in Bombay, Sholapur, and Nagpur. The government of India then banned the Communist Party and declared all Communist Party-controlled unions illegal. By crushing the trade union movement the government also expected to slow the momentum of the nationalistic movement. This period resulted in a major decline in the number of members of registered unions from 242,355 in 1929-30 to 208,071 in 1933-34.[12] Strike activity, rendered ineffective by economic conditions and bad organization, decreased from the all-time high figure of 31,647,404 man-days lost in 1928 to a mere 973,457 man-days lost in 1935. Participation in strikes declined, with only 114,217 workers involved in strikes in 1935 compared to the 406,851 workers involved in strikes in 1928 (see Table IV-2).

While militancy in the trade union movement continued to increase, especially in the Communist-controlled union of Ahmedabad, a peaceful and disciplined struggle to meet the same threat of unemployment was carried out under the leadership of the Textile Labour Association (TLA) formed in 1920. This union, guided by Mahatma Gandhi, was moderate in its approach and conducted negotiations with the employers. It also took a prag-

---

[11] *Ibid.*

[12] Karnik, *Indian Trade Unions*, p. 407.

TABLE IV-2
Strike Activity During 1928-1935

Year	No. of Stoppages	No. of Workers Involved	Man-days Lost
1928	203	506,851	31,647,404
1929	141	531,059	12,165,691
1930	148	196,301	2,261,731
1931	166	203,008	2,408,123
1932	118	128,099	1,922,437
1933	146	164,938	2,160,961
1934	159	220,808	4,775,559
1935	145	114,217	973,457

Source: Karnik, *Indian Trade Unions*, p. 409.

matic approach toward the introduction of rationalism by reaching mutual agreements and providing for a certain number of controls and safeguards to protect the interests of the workers. A landmark agreement between the TLA and the employers was made on the issue of rationalization, providing for mutual sharing of the gains of rationalization, a joint committee to supervise and regulate the working of the agreement, and for final and binding arbitration in case of conflict in the committee.

Because the unions had close political affilations with various segments of the nationalist movement during this period, changes in the political situation of the country played a major role in the growth and development of the trade union movement. The Government of India Act of 1935 granted provincial autonomy, and gave labor the right to be represented in the legislative assemblies. The INC, the major national political party at the time, decided to contest the election held in 1937. The party was sympathetic to the workers' cause, and its election manifesto included a clear-cut labor policy. The major aims of the labor policy were to secure international standards of working conditions for Indian workers and to provide suitable mechanisms for solving industrial disputes.

The INC won the elections and congress ministries were formed in seven out of nine provinces. These events coincided with the beginning of economic recovery in India and abroad. The higher economic and political expectations of the workers, however, were frustrated by the lack of trade union freedom and commensurate economic progress. The number of industrial disputes suddenly increased as a result. In 1937, the total number of man-days lost jumped to 8,982,257 from 973,457 in 1935 (see Table IV-3). The figure further increased to 9,198,708 in 1938 but there was a substantial decline in 1939.

TABLE IV-3
Industrial Disputes in India
During 1935-1939

Year	No. of Stoppages	No. of Workers Involved	Man-days Lost
1935	145	114,217	973,457
1936	157	169,029	5,358,062
1937	379	647,801	8,982,257
1938	399	401,075	9,198,708
1939	406	409,075	4,992,795

Source: Karnik, *Indian Trade Unions*, p. 409.

Important pieces of legislation passed during this period include the Shops and Establishments Act of 1939 and the Bombay Industrial Disputes Act of 1938, which was enacted by the government of the Province of Bombay. The first act was intended to give protection to workers in shops and commercial establishments, and the second act introduced the principle of compulsory adjudication of industrial disputes and prohibited strikes and lockouts under certain circumstances. Even though these laws were local in nature, they became catalysts for nationwide laws along similar lines. Another major legislative act was the Payment of Wages Act. Before it was enacted, the payment of wages to workers was irregular; fines had been imposed on the workers, and unauthorized deductions had been made from time to time by the employers, all of which lead to strikes and discontented workers. The Royal Commission on Labour recommended the introduction of a law to regulate deductions from wages and fix the periods between payment of wages. The Payment of Wages Act, passed in 1936, came into effect on February 28, 1937, and has continued in force to this day, albeit with several amendments.

During the period of setbacks for labor unions and early during their revival, the membership in registered unions declined. In 1933-34, however, after the unity moves began, membership increased again (see Table IV-4). The most marked growth both in number of unions and in membership occurred in the period from 1937 to 1940 when total registered membership increased from 261,047 in 1936-37 to 511,138 in 1939-40. Thus, this period helped to establish a pattern of growth in the movement and introduced to it a growing degree of maturity. It also strengthened the political nature of trade unions in the country, a phenomenon which evidenced itself in the greater ideological demarcations between unions and in the evolution of other major trade union federations throughout the next ten years.

TABLE IV-4
Registered Trade Unions in India
1929-30 to 1939-40

Year	No. of Registered Unions	No. of Registered Unions Submitting Returns	No. of Members
1929-30	104	90	242,355
1930-31	119	106	219,115
1931-32	131	121	235,693
1932-33	170	147	237,369
1933-34	191	160	208,071
1934-35	213	183	284,918
1935-36	241	205	268,326
1936-37	271	228	261,047
1937-38	420	343	390,112
1938-39	562	394	399,159
1939-40	667	450	511,138

Source: Karnik, *Indian Trade Unions*, p. 407.

The World War II Period—1939-1947

The Second World War, which began in 1939, brought the differences between the Communist Party faction in the AITUC and the mainstream nationalist faction out into the open. The various political factions within the reunited AITUC were already struggling for control of the organization. The Communists, guided by Moscow, condemned the war and opposed India's participation in it. This was because early in the war efforts, Soviet Russia and Nazi Germany were cooperating against the Western countries, including Great Britain. The INC also opposed India's inclusion in the war because the British had included India without consulting the Indian political parties. In mid-1941, however, when the pact between Soviet Russia and Nazi Germany ended, the Indian Communists reversed their opposition to the war on orders from the British Communist Party and Soviet Russia. Putting their political goals ahead of the interests of the labor movement, they advised the workers to moderate their demands and increase production.

The INC continued to oppose the war efforts and launched a massive "noncooperation" movement in 1942. The workers joined the movement, but the government cracked down and imprisoned practically all the important leaders of the INC, as well as its members in the AITUC, and the nationalist union leaders. The Communists consolidated their hold over the AITUC with the tacit backing of the British.

Meanwhile, in 1941, part of the INC faction that had unconditionally endorsed India's participation in the war but had failed to impose its views on the AITUC broke away and formed the Indian Federation of Labour (IFL). The IFL strongly supported British government and received financial assistance from the British. This was fatal to the growth of the federation, for it was discredited by the working class; it merged with the Hind Mazdoor Panchayat in December 1948 and was later to become the Hind Mazdoor Sabha (HMS).[13]

In 1945, after the war had ended, the imprisoned INC leaders were released, but by that time the AITUC was controlled totally by Communists. Realizing the futility of any efforts to persuade the Communists to subscribe to a united trade union policy, the INC decided to initiate action for the formation of a new body that would genuinely represent the interests of the working class in India. The result of these efforts, the Indian National Trade Union Congress (INTUC), was formed by the INC in May 1947. Since its formation, the INTUC has remained closely affiliated with the Congress Party.

Industrial disputes during this period were governed by the political environment. The number of workers involved in strike activity declined in 1941 to 291,054, the lowest figure in the decade, primarily because of widespread repression by the British government of India. The number of man-days lost in 1941 was 3,330,503, almost half the number lost in the preceeding year. Strike activity in 1942 jumped back to higher levels, stimulated by the strong, nationalist-led "Quit India" movement (see Table

---

[13] Ramanujam, *The Story of Indian Labour*, p. 52.

IV-5). Workers had higher expectations in the years preceding and following independence in 1947, and this also led to greater numbers of stoppages, workers involved, and man-days lost. The number of unions and the membership in registered unions grew at a more regular pace until 1944-45, but in the periods from 1946 to 1947 and from 1947 to 1948, the number of unions and their memberships grew at a rate of almost 50 percent per year (see Table IV-6). By the time of independence, the trade union movement had gained significant acceptance and recognition in the industrial and political life of India.

TABLE IV-5

Industrial Disputes in India

(1940-1947)

Year	No. of Stoppages	No. of Workers Involved	Man-days Lost
1940	322	452,539	7,577,281
1941	359	291,054	3,330,503
1942	694	772,653	5,779,965
1943	716	525,088	2,342,287
1944	658	550,015	3,447,306
1945	820	747,530	4,054,499
1946	1,629	1,961,948	12,717,762
1947	1,811	1,840,784	16,562,666

Source: Karnik, *Indian Trade Unions*, p. 409.

TABLE IV-6

Registered Trade Unions in India

(1939-40 to 1947-48)

Year	No. of Registered Unions	No. of Registered Unions Submitting Returns	No. of Members
1939-40	667	450	511,138
1940-41	727	483	513,832
1941-42	747	455	573,520
1942-43	693	489	685,299
1943-44	761	563	780,967
1944-45	865	573	889,388
1945-46	1,087	585	864,031
1946-47	1,225	998	1,331,962
1947-48	2,766	1,620	1,662,929

Source: Karnik, *Indian Trade Unions*, p. 407.

The Post-Independence Period—1947-1981

After independence, the major common denominator, the struggle for independence, was removed as the focus of trade union activities. No longer restrained by the cause that had previously united them, ideological differences between the trade unions began to surface again; as a result, a number of major new trade union congresses were organized.

The federation which suffered most from the partition of the country into India and Pakistan was the IFL. Most of its members were either in the area that became Pakistan or had migrated to Pakistan. Its strength and influence weakened, the IFL merged in 1948 with a splinter group of the AITUC, the Hind Mazdoor Panchayat, and they formed a new organization, the Hind Mazdoor Sabha (HMS). The rise of the HMS represented the emergence of a new force amid the politically-affiliated INTUC and AITUC. Furthermore, the HMS retained as a basic principle the independence of trade unions from the government, employers, and political parties. In December 1948, when the HMS was started, it had 427 unions representing a membership of 606,372.[14] It took an active part in the trade union movement in the 1950s and continues to be a major central trade union federation today.

About the same time that the HMS was formed, another central organization, the United Trade Union Congress (UTUC), came into existence. The UTUC was formed in April 1949 by dissidents from the AITUC. It had a membership of 384,962 in 1951.[15] The UTUC was active predominantly in the states of Kerala and West Bengal and it maintained that strength in the succeeding years.

The course of the trade union movement in the decades following independence was more diverse. Trade union activity continued on and off. Political affiliations usually governed the stands the central trade unions took on issues. The unions came to accept the value of voluntary arbitration. The Code of Discipline, which evolved in 1958 and was accepted by both employers and workers organizations, declared that disputes be settled by representations, negotiations, and, in the last resort, by arbitration. Employers, however, did not implement the Code of Discipline with total commitment. In the years between 1948 and 1971

---

[14] Giri, *Labour Problems in Indian Industry*, pp. 29-30.

[15] *Ibid.*, pp. 31, 45.

the number of unions jumped from 3,150 to 21,933, with membership increasing from 1,960,107 to 5,228,000 (see Table IV-7).

In spite of this large growth in the number of unions and the size of their membership, the nature of unions remained the same. Most unions in India today are either craft or plant unions. The average size of unions has declined steadily over the years (see Table IV-8). This decline is due primarily to the size of the country and the important role of local issues in most trade union disputes. Central trade unions counteract this trend to some extent by providing larger policy-level guidance, but the trend is unlikely to be reversed. Relatively industrialized states, and industries such as iron and steel, coal mining, textiles, chemicals,

TABLE IV-7

Registered Trade Unions in India

(1948-49 to 1971)

Year	No. of Registered Unions	No. of Registered Unions Submitting Returns	No. of Members
1948-49	3,150	1,848	1,960,107
1949-50	3,522	1,919	1,821,132
1950-51	3,766	2,002	1,756,971
1951-52	4,623	2,556	1,996,311
1952-53	4,934	2,718	2,099,003
1953-54	6,029	3,295	2,112,695
1954-55	6,658	3,545	2,170,450
1955-56	8,095	4,006	2,275,000
1956-57	8,554	4,399	2,377,000
1957-58	10,045	5,520	3,015,000
1958-59	10,228	6,040	3,647,000
1959-60	10,811	6,588	3,923,000
1960-61	11,312	6,813	4,013,000
1961-62	11,476	7,044	3,728,000
1962-63	11,827	7,521	3,682,000
1963-64	11,984	7,250	3,977,000
1964-65	13,023	7,543	4,466,000
1965	13,248	6,932	3,788,000
1966	14,686	7,244	4,392,000
1967	15,314	7,523	4,525,000
1968	16,716	8,851	5,121,000
1969	18,837	8,423	4,900,000
1970	20,681	8,537	4,887,000
1971	21,565	8,248	3,762,000

Source: Karnik, *Indian Trade Unions*, pp. 391, 407-408.

TABLE IV-8
Average Size of Unions in India

Year	Average Membership
1927-28	3,594
1935-36	1,309
1947-48	1,026
1951-52	781
1955-56	568
1960-61	589
1963-64	549
1964-65	592

Source: Karnik, *Indian Trade Unions*, p. 329.

food and tobacco processing, and railways have the strongest unions.[16]

A major spurt in trade union activity took place in the late 1960s and early 1970s. One major strike was conducted in 1974 in the railways; the strikers were severely repressed by the government. The strike failed after a few days but it hardened the attitude of the government toward totally free trade union activity. This attitude was further reflected in the total clamp down on trade unions during Indira Gandhi's emergency rule from June 1975 to March 1977.

During Janata rule a wave of industrial strikes occurred, attributed to the lifting of many restrictions by the government. After Mrs. Gandhi's election in 1980, however, government restrictions increased, resulting in a decline in the number of strikes in the country.

MAJOR TRADE UNIONS AND CONFEDERATIONS

The current total trade union membership in India is estimated at between 4 and 5 million workers. Trade union members represent practically all industries, excluding agricultural workers, workers in cottage industries, employees in small shops and establishments, and domestic workers. Workers in the manufacturing industries account for the largest membership, about 43.9 percent (see Table IV-9). Railways, mining and quarrying, plantation, and commercial workers also contribute a significant percentage of total trade union membership. Many white-collar professionals are also organized; and unions are prevalent in the

---

[16] A. P. Coldrick and P. Jones, *International Directory of the Trade Union Movement* (New York: Facts on File, Inc., 1979), pp. 467-468.

larger wholesale and retail trade organizations, in banks, insurance companies, government, and among medical and paramedical professions.

TABLE IV-9

Number and Membership of Unions Submitting Returns by Branches of Economic Activity, 1974

Economic Activity	Number of Unions Reporting	Membership	
		Number (in thousands)	Percent
Agriculture, forestry, fishing, etc.	150	161	3.8
Mining and quarrying	113	362	8.6
Manufacturing	2,537	1,812	43.2
Construction	186	130	3.1
Electricity, gas, & water	160	160	3.8
Commerce	866	300	7.2
Transportation & communications	561	838	20.0
Services	792	248	5.9
Others	298	185	4.4
Total	5,662	4,196	100.0

Source: *Pocket Book of Labour Statistics, 1978* (Labour Bureau, Ministry of Labour, Government of India), p. 127.

Most central trade union confederations in India emerged from within the AITUC as a result either of conflicting ideologies or of political factionalism. The AITUC, as mentioned earlier, was formed not for the conventional reason of uniting labor unions of similar ideologies and interests, but for the purpose of selecting representatives to the ILO.

Today, the major central trade union organizations still have relatively little participation in local and plant level union affairs, serving mainly as coordination agencies for national trade union policy.

The roles filled today by the major central trade union organizations, the backgrounds of which were discussed earlier in the chapter, are explained below.

The Indian National Trade Union Congress (INTUC)

The INTUC, formed in 1947 to provide an alternative to the Communist-controlled AITUC, is closely affiliated with the INC, the ruling party for most of the years since independence. Today it is the largest central trade union organization with a claimed membership of over 3.2 million workers in 3,108 unions across the country.[17] It has branches in most states of the union and has set up industrial federations in such industries as cement, defense, electricity, metal, Indian government presses, municipal and local bodies, chemicals, port and dock, food and drink, insurance, mining, paper, petroleum, sugar, transport, cantonment, banking, post and telegraph, plantations, textiles, railways, and building and construction.

Because of its close ties with the ruling party and the government, the INTUC has never taken a very militant role in the trade union movement. It has, in fact, attempted to moderate the trade union activity of its members so that such activity would not embarrass the government. The INTUC has opposed the use of strikes and labor violence and it favors settling labor disputes through arbitration, wage boards, tribunals, and by exercising its political influence with the government. After the 1977 defeat of the Congress government and the election of an opposition government at the Center and in several states, the INTUC increased its industrial action and strikes in opposition to the Janata government's policy. The organization has reintroduced restraint in its labor activities now that the Congress (Indira) Party is back in power. The close relationship between the INTUC and Mrs. Gandhi's Congress Party is exemplified by the fact that the president of the INTUC was appointed a minister in her government in January 1980.

The INTUC was a founding member of the International Confederation of Free Trade Unions (ICFTU) and has remained an active affiliate.

The All-India Trade Union Congress (AITUC)

The oldest and the second largest central trade union organization in India, the AITUC has for most of its lifetime been dominated by Communists. The AITUC closely follows the Communist Party line and its top leaders have been prominent members of the Communist Party of India. When the international Communist movement split into Russian and Chinese factions, the Communist Party of India also split into the Moscow-oriented Communist Party of India (CPI) and the Communist Party of

---

[17] G. Ramanujam, *INTUC Report, January 1975 to October 1978* (New Delhi: INTUC, 1978), Appendix—A (ii), p. 4.

India/Marxist (CPI/M), which looked to China for ideological guidance. The CPI tried to maintain the unity of the AITUC, but that was not acceptable to the Marxists. The CPI/M-controlled faction of the AITUC broke away and formed a new central organization, the Centre of Indian Trade Unions (CITU), in May 1970.

The AITUC claims a membership of over 2.5 million in 2,805 affiliated unions, with 18 regional branches.[18] It is especially strong in the states of West Bengal and Kerala, with major strongholds in the steel, defense, engineering, and communications industries, and among white-collar workers. In the past, the AITUC has aggressively supported workers' rights and demands. It advocates the free use of strikes and other labor actions as means of rectifying labor grievances and protesting government policies. In line with the policies of the Communist Party of India, which aligned itself with Mrs. Gandhi during her "emergency rule," the AITUC tempered its opposition to government policies during that period.

The AITUC affiliated itself with the World Federation of Trade Unions (WFTU) at that organization's foundation in 1945 and has remained an active member to date.

The Hind Mazdoor Sabha (HMS)

The HMS was established in 1948 by the Socialist faction of the INC. It remained affiliated to the Rohia and Praja Socialist Parties. When the Socialist Party splintered into several other parties, the political ties of the HMS became unclear. Several of its top leaders aligned themselves with Mrs. Gandhi's Congress Party and some supported the Janata Party in 1977. A faction of the HMS broke away in 1962 and formed the Hind Mazdoor Panchayat (HMP), which was associated with the Samyukta Socialist Party. This union congress was active mainly in the Bombay area. The Hind Mazdoor Panchayat and the HMS merged in February 1979 and kept the name Hind Mazdoor Sabha.[19] This union claims a membership of over one million members in 525 affiliated unions.[20] It is strong in the transportation, railway,

---

[18] Coldrick and Jones, *International Directory of the Trade Union Movement*, p. 471.

[19] *International Union of Food and Allied Workers Associations News Bulletin*, No. 56, 1979, p. 6.

[20] Coldrick and Jones, *International Directory of the Trade Union Movement*, p. 468.

shipping, plantation, and steel industries. The HMS is opposed to compulsory arbitration and upholds the independence of trade unions and the right to strike.

The HMS is affiliated to the ICFTU and participates in its activities.

The Centre of Indian Trade Unions (CITU)

The CITU was formed in 1970 by the Communist Party (Marxist) after the division in the Communist Party of India. The organization claims a membership of over 1.1 million workers in 2,231 affiliated unions.[21] The CITU has been very strong in Kerala, West Bengal, and Tripura, but its influence in other regions is minimal. The leadership of the CITU is making a concerted effort to increase the centre's activities in the Hindi speaking areas of the north. The union is strongly opposed to government interference in industrial relations. It favors strikes and labor action as methods for settling worker disputes with employers. The CITU has remained, in spite of its close ties with Communist Party Marxists, independent of political influence, and it has conducted strikes and protests against the government in West Bengal, which is led by its own party.

The CITU, even though not fully affiliated to the WFTU, participated as an observer group at the WFTU conference held in Prague, Czechoslovakia, and it may affiliate if invited.[22]

The Bhartiya Mazdoor Sangh (BMS)

The BMS was formed in 1955 by the Jan Sangh, a militant nationalist party, so that it could introduce its ideology to the trade union movement. The trade union base has also helped the party to create a cadre of indoctrinated workers. The aim of the BMS is to counteract the communist influence over workers. Its primary strength lies among the white-collar workers in banking, municipal services, and the retail trade. The union claims a membership of about one million. The union's ties with the Jan Sangh, now known as the Bhartiya Janata Party and its militant volunteer group, the Rashtriya Swayamsevak Sangh, remain strong.

The BMS is not affiliated to any International Trade Secretariat.

---

[21] *Ibid.*, p. 472.

[22] P. Ramamurti, *General Report: Centre of Indian Trade Unions, 4th Annual Conference* (New Delhi: CITU, 1979), p. 29.

The United Trade Union Congress (UTUC)

The Trotskyite members of the Communist Party formed the UTUC in 1949. The organization is extremely leftist-oriented and has promoted the use of strikes as a major tool for the Indian trade union movement. The UTUC opposes the government's arbitration system, claiming that it is biased in favor of the employers. This trade union congress, like other leftist organizations, remains strong primarily in the states of West Bengal and Kerala. In the early 1970s, the UTUC split into two groups and both groups claim to be the "real" UTUC. Both are located in Calcutta, with one's offices located at Lenin Sarni and the other's at Ganguly Street. The claimed membership of the UTUC (Lenin Sarni) is 944,753 and that of the UTUC (Ganguly Street) is 362,087. The figures recognized by the government, however, as in the case of other unions, are much lower for both groups.

The UTUC is not affiliated with any major International Trade Secretariat, but it has been sympathetic to the policies of the WFTU.

In addition to these six major central trade union organizations, a few others have come into existence in the last decade. Prominent among them are the National Labour Organization (NLO) and the National Front of Indian Trade Unions (NFITU). A major affiliate of the NLO, the Textile Labour Association, Ahmedabad, is considered one of the strongest and best-conducted union organizations in the country. It claims a membership of 277,714. The NFITU is affiliated to the World Confederation of Labour (WCL) and has a membership of 575,384.[23]

Until 1968, the government of India conducted biannual verification of union membership claims and recognized the INTUC, the AITUC, the UTUC, and the HMS as the four largest central trade union organizations. After this verification process was stopped, these four organizations continued to enjoy government recognition as central trade union confederations. As the structure and membership of these confederations changed, the trade unions pressured the government to verify membership claims and set up a new standard of recognition for central trade union organizations. In 1979, the government revised its previous criterion of a membership numbering at least 100,000 to a membership of

---

[23] *Ibid.*, p. 2.

at least 800,000.[24] According to this new standard, the list of recognized central trade union organizations is limited to five: the INTUC, the AITUC, the HMS, the CITU, and the BMS. Table IV-10 gives comparative data on India's major central trade union organizations.

TRADE UNION FINANCES

The primary source of income for Indian trade unions is the membership dues. The amount of these dues varies among unions and depends upon the services provided by the union, the strength of the union, and periodic financial needs arising from strikes or arbitration. Other sources of union income are donations, proceeds from the sale of union publications, and special collections. The financial position of most unions, with a few exceptions, remains weak. Most union failures can be linked directly to financial problems. As can be seen from Table IV-11, the average income and expenditure of unions in 1970 was very low, at Rs. 4720 and Rs. 3947 respectively, and these figures have hardly kept pace with inflation, let alone grown in real terms.

These numbers appear even lower in light of the fact that most of the expenditures and income are accounted for by the larger unions, which are fewer in number than small unions. Smaller unions suffer from the vicious circle of a lack of funds that prevents organization of a larger number of workers and small membership, which results in a poor financial situation.

The low wages paid to Indian workers, which make membership contributions to unions a financial burden, are one reason for this situation. In multi-union plants, the competition for the workers' membership reduces the dues required for membership to the lowest level prescribed by law. Both the check-off system and union shop are illegal and this further reduces both motivation for membership and regular payment of dues.

The weak financial condition of the unions severely restricts the scope of their activities; they spend only about 6.2 percent of their incomes on educational and welfare activities. Lack of welfare activities has been a major reason for the comparatively meager contact between workers and their unions.[25]

---

[24] "Government recognizes INTUC as the premier centre?," *The Indian Worker*, May 21, 1979, p. 1.

[25] Karnik, *Indian Trade Unions*, pp. 328-329.

TABLE IV-10
Central Trade Union Organizations in India

Name of Organization	Membership Claimed (Dec. 31, 1977)	Membership Accepted by Govt. of India	Political Affiliation	International Affiliation
The Indian National Trade Union Congress 1-B, Maulana Azad Road New Delhi 110001	3,372,875	2,388,451	Congress (Indira)	ICFTU
The All-India Trade Union Congress 24, Canning Lane New Delhi 110001	1,800,000	1,307,471	Communist Party of India (CPI)	WFTU
The Hind Mazdoor Sabha 12, Chelmsford Road New Delhi 110001	1,200,000	1,074,080	Various Socialist Parties	ICFTU
The Bhartiya Mazdoor Sangh 23, Vithalbhai Patel House, Rafi Marg New Delhi 110001	1,102,183	859,200	Bhartiya Janata Party (Jan Sangh)	None
The Centre of Indian Trade Unions 6, Talkatora Road New Delhi 110001	1,500,000	817,805	Communist Party of India/Marxist (CPI/M)	None
The United Trade Union Congress (Lenin Sarni) 77/2/1, Lenin Sarni Calcutta	944,753	384,564	Revolutionary Socialist Party (Trotsky-ites)	None

TABLE IV-10 (Continued)

Name of Organization	Membership Claimed (Dec. 31, 1977)	Membership Accepted by Govt. of India	Political Affiliation	International Affiliation
The United Trade Union Congress 249, B.B. Ganguli Street Calcutta 700012	362,087	173,571	Revolutionary Socialist Party (Trotskyites)	None
The National Labour Organization Gandhi Mazdoor Sevalaya Bhadra, Ahmedabad	277,714	202,965	Janata Party	None
The National Front of Indian Trade Unions 2, Jawaharlal Nehru Road Calcutta	575,384	224,520	None	WCL
The Trade Union Coordination Committee 52/7 B.B. Ganguli Street Calcutta 700012	153,635	33,931	None	None

Source: Industrial Research Unit files.

TABLE IV-11
*Average Annual Income and Expenditure of
Trade Unions in India*

Year	Average Membership Per Union	Average Income Per Union (Rs.)	Average Expenditure Per Union (Rs.)
1951-52	781	2,026	1,806
1956-57	540	1,826	1,636
1961-62	561	2,461	2,176
1964-65	594	3,195	2,751
1968	579	3,914	3,493
1970	600	4,720	3,947

Source: *Indian Labour Year Book,* 1974 (Simla: Labour Bureau, Ministry of Labour, Government of India, 1977), pp. 61-62, 74.

The trade union movement will have to introduce reforms such as acceptance of the largest union in a plant as the sole bargaining agent in order to increase the credibility of local unions and their effectiveness in labor disputes. An effective union would probably make workers aware of the importance of membership contributions; such a realization would lead to greater financial strength for the unions.

UNION LEADERSHIP

The trade union movement in India was led at first by leaders of the independence movement, and since independence it has been led by politically-oriented "outsiders." Most Indian trade union leaders have neither a working class background nor significant trade union experience. Thus, a trade union leader may be looking for political power and status. This issue has caused great controversy in the Indian trade union movement. Those opposed to the outsiders consider them more prone to cause disturbances in industrial peace without necessarily taking the legitimate interests of the workers into account. The presence of outsiders has also led to inter-union rivalry and to political power struggles within a union.

Multiple unions have resulted mainly from the desire of political outsiders to establish unions of their own with a view toward increasing their political influence. The fragmentation that occurred soon after independence in the central trade union organizations was primarily due to the political differences between trade union leaders; this problem continues to date.

The important role of outsiders in Indian unions can be explained by the generally low level of worker awareness, the widespread illiteracy, the ignorance of labor laws, and the lack of knowledge of English, the working language of business and industry. These factors have been major obstacles to the emergence of strong inside union leadership. The weak financial position of unions has prevented them from hiring professionals and an increasingly complex arbitration and adjudication system has forced most unions to depend upon outsiders. The current labor law is also liberal in that it allows outsiders in unions. Under the Trade Unions Act of 1926, any person not actually engaged in or employed by the industry concerned is considered an outsider. Section 22 of that act requires that at least 50 percent of the officers of a registered trade union be actively engaged in or employed by an industry to which the union belongs.[26] Worker participation in unions run by outsiders has remained low. Improved worker education and trade union training are urgently needed if the trend of outsider control of trade unions is to be reversed and the participation of workers in their unions is to be increased.

INTERNATIONAL AFFILIATIONS

The Indian trade union movement has been involved in International Trade Secretariats and global labor organizations for as long as such organizations have existed. India was a founding member of the ILO; in fact, central trade union organizations were started in India for the purpose of participation in the ILO. (See Appendix D for a list of ILO conventions that have been ratified by India and Appendix E for ILO recommendations that have been fully implemented by India.) The AITUC has been affiliated to the WFTU since 1945, the year in which the WFTU was established. Similarly, the INTUC and the HMS were founding members of the ICFTU and they participated in the preparatory conference in Geneva in June 1949 and the Inaugural Conference in London in November 1949.[27] The INTUC has been an active participant in ICFTU activities since then.

The International Trade Secretariats (ITSs) have several affiliates among the Indian trade unions and have conducted programs on worker education and trade union training. The level of these

---

[26] *Report of the National Commission on Labour* (New Delhi: Ministry of Labour, Employment and Rehabilitation, 1969), p. 288.

[27] Ramanujam, *The Story of Indian Labour*, pp. 54, 77.

activities, however, has been relatively modest, primarily due to the weakness of Indian trade unions and the multiplicity of unions in each industry, which makes the task of organizing workers in a specific industry almost impossible. Several secretariats have held regional conferences in India, but basically, their foothold in India has been weak.

Low wages, high unemployment, and the low level of industrialization in India have led to Indian trade unions having a totally different set of priorities from the secretariats, whose membership lies mainly in the industrialized West. Thus, it is not surprising that the interests of the secretariats and their Indian affiliates conflict on several issues. Whereas the main concerns of the secretariats are higher wages and worker safety, local Indian trade unions give the problem of unemployment a high priority. Trade barriers and import restrictions that an ITS affiliate in a developed country could impose would probably lead to unemployment in developing countries. This obvious conflict of interest, as well as the fact that most secretariats owe their existence to larger unions in the West, severely hinders ITS campaigns in developing countries like India.

A specific example of this conflict of interest can be found in the opposition of both Indian trade unions and the government of India to the International Transport Workers' Federation (ITF) campaign against flag-of-convenience ships, which involves the boycott of ships not paying minimum wages set by the ITF. In 1973, the ITF negotiated rates with the International Shipping Federation (ISF), a group of individual shipowners and companies employing Asian crews. The ISF agreed to compensate Asian seafarers at the rate of £48 per month, the minimum established by the ILO at the time despite the fact that national seamen's unions were demanding less than that rate.[28]

Later, however, when the contract came up for renegotiation in October 1973, the government of India forbade domestic shipowners on its national maritime board from offering more than £32 per month and threatened to withhold labor supply from companies that employed crews at ILO rates. The government of India, supported by local ITF affiliates, considered this a move of "enlightened self-interest." The government and the Indian unions felt that in the face of growing unemployment in Britain and elsewhere in the West, Indian seamen would be laid off once

---

[28] "Shipping: wage spiral," _The Economic Times_, July 31, 1973, p. 1.

they lost their attractiveness to shipowners (i.e. low wages). They also felt that a higher wage for Indian seamen on foreign flag carriers was likely to precipitate a demand for higher wages by seamen working with Indian ships. This, they felt, would have serious repercussions for the Indian shipping industry and employment therein.[29]

Protests against the ITF's policy of boycotting ships that employed Indian seamen resulted in the suspension of the National Union of Seafarers of India (NUSI) from the ITF.[30] The NUSI, with 24,000 members, was the largest ITF affiliate in the Indian shipping industry, and the suspension has weakened the ITF's representation of seamen from developing countries.

The ITSs' campaign against multinational corporations is relatively weak in India. This is primarily due to the low profile of Indian subsidiaries of major multinationals and their relative independence of operations. Only a few cases of International Trade Secretariats providing help in organizing to Indian affiliates are known, one such case being the International Metalworkers' Federation's (IMF) campaign against the SKF. Philips and Siemens have had some impact on Indian trade unions even though the issues involved were strictly local in nature.

Table IV-12 shows the Indian affiliates of some major ITSs.

---

[29] "British wages for seamen opposed," *The Overseas Hindustan Times,* November 23, 1978, p. 5.

[30] International Transport Workers' Federation, *Report on Activities 1977-79,* ITF 33rd Congress, July 17-25, 1980, p. 25.

TABLE IV-12

The International Trade Secretariats in India

International Trade Secretariat	Indian Affiliates	Membership
International Federation of Building and Woodworkers (IFBWW)	Building Mazdoor Union	682
	Indian National Building and Construction Workers Federation	NA
International Federation of Chemical, Energy and General Workers' Unions (ICEF)	Indian National Cement and Allied Workers Federation (INTUC)	93,000
	Glass, Potteries and Ceramic Industries Unions (INTUC)	31,113
	Indian National Papermill Workers Federation (INTUC)	30,000
	Rubber Industry Unions (INTUC)	12,934
	Services, Trade and Vocation Unions (INTUC)	6,128
	The All-India Federation of Chemical Workers	65,000
	The All-India Federation of Petroleum Workers	25,000
	Central Council of Chemical, Petroleum and General Workers' Unions (HMS)	50,000
	The Government of India Press Workers Union	10,000
International Federation of Commercial, Clerical, Professional and Technical Employees (FIET)	All-India Bank Employees' Federation	17,609
	All-India Life Insurance Employees' Federation	11,650
	All-India Reserve Bank Karmchari Federation	1,907

TABLE IV-12 (Continued)

International Trade Secretariat	Indian Affiliates	Membership
	Indian National Commercial and Salaried Employees' Federation	46,336
	Indian National Commercial and Salaried Employees Association	35,131
International Secretariat of Entertainment Trade Unions (ISETU)	Indian Motion Picture Employees' Union	NA
International Graphical Federation (IGF)	Indian Federation of Graphical Workers	1,385
	Press Mazdoor Sabha	1,550
International Metalworkers' Federation (IMF)	Central Steel and Engineering Committee	212,500
	Indian National Metalworkers' Union (INTUC)	538,851
Miners' International Federation	Indian National Mineworkers' Federation	NA
International Federation of Petroleum and Chemical Workers (IFPCW)	National Federation of Petroleum Workers	25,000
	Association of Chemical Workers	NA
	National Association of Indian Oil Employees	NA
	Synthetic Drugs Employees' Union	NA
	Rubber Factory Workers' Union	NA
	Indian National Chemical Workers' Federation	80,000

International Federation of Plantation, Agricultural and Allied Workers (IFPAAW)	Indian National Plantation Workers' Federation	31,000
	Neelamalai Plantation Workers' Union	24,689
	Sakhar Kamgar Sabha Shrirampur Union	2,678
	The Estates Staff's Union of South India	2,917
	West Bengal Cha Mazdoor Sabha	20,079
Postal, Telegraph and Telephone International (PTTI)	National Federation of Post and Telegraph Employees	120,000
	Posts and Telegraphs Industrial Workers Union	10,000
	Posts and Telegraphs Mazdoor Union	3,000
	Indian Telephone Industries Employees' Union	9,000
	Federation of National Post and Telecommunications Organizations	60,000
International Federation of Free Teachers' Unions (IFFTU)	Secondary School Teachers Union, Delhi	NA
International Textile, Garment and Leather Workers' Federation (ITGLWF)	Hind Mazdoor Sabha	92,780
	Indian National Leatherworkers' Federation	8,155
	Indian National Textile Workers' Federation	415,836
	National Labour Organization Textile Section	180,000
International Transport Workers' Federation (ITF)	All India Railwaymen's Federation	50,000
	The Maritime Union of India	5,310
	Calcutta Port Shramik Union	7,500
	The Indian Flight Navigators' Guild	58
	Indian Flight Engineers' Association	118

TABLE IV-12 (Continued)

International Trade Secretariat	Indian Affiliates	Membership
	Transport and Dock Workers' Union	12,600
	National Union of Seamen of India	10,728
	National Union of Seafarers of India	24,000
	National Federation of Indian Railwaymen	300,000
	Air India Cabin Crew Association	800
	Air India Employees' Guild	2,000
Public Services International (PSI)	All India Cantonment Board Employees Federation	NA
	India National Defense Workers' Federation	NA
	Indian National Electricity Workers' Federation	NA
	Indian National Municipal and Local Bodies Workers' Federation	NA
International Federation of Air Line Pilots' Associations (IFALPA)	Indian Pilots Guild	173
World Federation of Trade Unions (WFTU)	All India Trade Union Congress	1,307,471
International Confederation of Free Trade Unions (ICFTU)	Hind Mazdoor Sabha	1,191,416
	Indian National Trade Union Congress	3,259,770
World Confederation of Labour (WCL)	National Front of Indian Trade Unions	224,520

Sources: Industrial Research Unit files.

CHAPTER V

Labor Legislation and Administration

The evolution of labor legislation in India closely followed the growth of the trade union movement. Indian labor legislation has been patterned after British models ever since the passage of the first Indian labor law, the Indian Trade Unions Act, in 1926. Because of the close ties between the trade union movement and the struggle for national independence, the labor laws of the period before independence were biased in favor of the employers and sought to curb the trade union movement. After independence, both constitutional and statutory bases were established for labor legislation. The constitution provided a number of guidelines for the enactment of labor welfare legislation and contained directives to provide for equal pay for equal work for both men and women, minimum age requirements, and decent wages and working conditions. The scope of these labor laws has, however, remained limited to the organized sector, at least in practice. Over the last three or four decades, the state has come to occupy the functions normally fulfilled by trade unions. Voluntary arbitration and mediation, rather than collective bargaining between the workers and their employers, have played major roles in the settlement of labor problems.

This chapter examines the development of labor legislation in India, discusses the major labor laws and their impact on trade union activity, and outlines the administrative structure under which the government implements these laws.

DEVELOPMENT OF LABOR LAWS IN INDIA

The process of industrial development in India began in the second half of the nineteenth century, but it was not until World War I that Indian workers achieved any legal rights. The first labor case in India, that of Buckingham Mills versus Madras Labour Union, was heard in 1920. The employers sued the union for damages and sought an injunction against its activities. The High Court of Madras treated the union as an illegal conspiracy and granted an injunction against union activities. This led to protests by the Indian trade union movement and the British Trade Union Congress.[1] The pressure of these protests resulted in the Indian Trade Union Act, enacted by the government of India in 1926. The act, for the first time, provided for registration of unions and granted immunity from criminal prosecution to trade union leaders. This law thus provided legal recognition of the workers' right to organize and took the first step in the direction of regulation of the trade union movement as well as of employers' responses to union activities. The Trade Union Act of 1926, however, did not provide a system for the settlement of industrial disputes or for collective bargaining. Large scale strikes and consequent disruption of industrial peace led to the enactment of the Trade Disputes Act of 1929. This act made provisions for peaceful settlement of industrial disputes, required a fourteen-day notice from a union prior to a strike in a public utility, prohibited strikes that could cause severe hardships to the community, and declared sympathetic, general, and political strikes to be illegal.

This act, in practice, turned out to be of only marginal use. It was invoked on only five occasions, despite heavy union activity during the years from 1929 to 1936. Furthermore, it was superseded by the emergency provisions of the Defence of India Rules which had been promulgated after the start of the Second World War. These rules empowered the government "(i) to make general or special orders to prohibit strikes or lockouts in connection with trade disputes unless reasonable advance notice of intent was given; (ii) to refer any dispute to conciliation or adjudication; (iii) to prohibit strikes and lockouts during the conciliation or adjudication proceedings; (iv) to enforce conciliation or adjudication awards; and (v) to require employers to observe such terms and conditions as may be required." [2]

After the war, the government replaced the emergency provisions of the Defence of India Rules with the Industrial Disputes Act (1947) which combined the compulsory arbitration principles of the Defence of India Rules and the conciliation machinery and courts of inquiry system of the Trade Disputes Act of 1929. The

---

[1] Arjun P. Aggarwal, *Indian and American Labor Legislation and Practices* (New York: Asia Publishing House, 1966), p. 11.

[2] *Ibid.*, p. 13.

Industrial Disputes Act sought to ensure the workers a fair return for their services and to prevent the disruption of industrial peace. Earlier, in 1946, the government had enacted the Industrial Employment (Standing Orders) Act, which sought to regulate the terms and conditions of employment of workers in industry. The Industrial Disputes Act of 1947 and the Indian Trade Union Act of 1926, combined with the Industrial Employment (Standing Orders) Act of 1946, have continued, each with several amendments, to serve as the core of labor and industrial legislation in the country. Attempts to consolidate these three and several other laws into a comprehensive industrial relations law have been made, first in the form of the Trade Union Bill of 1950, and then in the Industrial Relations Bill of 1978. The Parliament passed neither of these bills, owing to a lack of agreement among labor unions, the employers, and the government; and labor legislation in India remains mired in a multiplicity of laws and rules that govern the relationship between trade unions and employers.

MAJOR LABOR LAWS OF INDIA

Legislative powers in India are shared by the union and the state governments in accordance with the division of legislative authority provided by the constitution. Legislative responsibilities are divided into three "lists": the union list, the concurrent list, and the state list. The Parliament has exclusive power to enact laws concerning matters on the union list, while the state legislatures have, with some exceptions, exclusive powers to enact laws relating to issues on the state list. The concurrent list contains subjects regarding which both the state and the union governments may pass laws. In cases of conflict between state laws and union laws, the union laws prevail. The subjects which pertain to labor in each list are enumerated in Table V-1.

As seen in the table, most laws relating to trade unions and industrial and labor disputes are on the concurrent list. Most industrial relations laws are passed by the Parliament; the states have enacted some labor laws, but most of them either are minor modifications of the central laws or are limited in scope.

Currently in force are over a hundred labor laws which have been enacted at both state and union levels. Appendix F contains a comprehensive list of important labor laws. The major laws with a national scope are examined in the following sections. State laws that supplement these acts do exist, but in cases of conflict, the national laws supersede the state laws.

TABLE V-1

Division of Legislative Authority in Labor Related Issues

Union List

1. Participation in international conferences, associations, and other bodies and implementation of decisions made thereat.
2. Major ports and port quarantine.
3. Regulation of labor and safety in mines and oil fields.
4. Industrial disputes concerning union employees.
5. Union agencies and institutions for
   a. professional, vocational, or technical training,
   b. the promotion of special studies or research.
6. Inquiries, surveys, and statistics for the purpose of any of the matters in the union list.
7. Railways.
8. Airways, aircraft and air navigation, air traffic and aerodromes, etc.
9. Post & telegraphs, telephones, wireless, broadcasting, etc.

State List

Relief of the disabled and unemployable.

Concurrent List

1. Economic and social planning.
2. Trade unions, industrial and labor disputes.
3. Social security and social insurance, employment and unemployment.
4. Welfare of labor, including conditions of work, provident fund, employers' liability, workmen's compensation, invalidity and old age pension, and maternity benefits.
5. Vocational and technical training of labor.
6. Factories.
7. Inquiries and statistics for purposes of any of the matters specified in the concurrent list and the state list.

Source: *Indian Labour Year Book, 1974* (Simla: Labour Bureau, Ministry of Labour, Government of India, 1977), p. 155.

The Indian Trade Unions Act of 1926

This act, which was amended in 1928, 1942, 1947, and 1960, confers a legal status on registered trade unions and provides immunity from civil and criminal liability to trade union executives and members who participate in bona fide trade union activities. The main provisions of this act relate to: (1) registration of unions; (2) rights and privileges of unions; and (3) obligations and liabilities of registered trade unions.

Any seven or more members of a union may apply for registration of the union under this act. After verifying their compliance with the rules for registration under the act, the registrar of trade unions is required to issue to the union a certificate of registration. At least half the total number of office bearers of a registered trade union must actually be engaged in the industry to which the union belongs. There is also a minimum subscription fee of twenty-five Paise per month per member of the trade union.[3]

Besides granting immunity from criminal prosecution to union leaders for genuine trade union activities, this act bars any civil suit against any trade union and its officers for any action just because "such an act induces some other person to break a contract of employment, or that it is in interference with the trade, business, or employment of some other person or with the right of some other person to dispose of his capital or of his labour as he wills." [4] The act also declares that an agreement between members of a registered trade union cannot be declared illegal merely because an object of the agreement is in restraint of trade.

The act lays down the responsibilities of a registered trade union, stipulating that it will spend union funds only on authorized items, that it will maintain separate funds for political purposes, the money for which must be raised separately from money for union activities, and that it will continue to comply with all rules under the act.

The Industrial Disputes Act of 1947

This act has been amended fifteen times since it was originally passed in 1947. It is the most comprehensive law governing Indian industrial relations.[5] A major provision of the act was the establishment of machinery for the peaceful settlement of industrial disputes. It introduced the concept of compulsory arbitration and prohibited strikes without notice in public utility services. Two new institutions were provided for the first time: (1) works committees to promote relations between employers and workers, and (2) the Industrial Tribunal for the adjudication of industrial disputes.

The act defines "workmen" as all workers including technical staff and supervisory personnel who earn a salary of up to Rs. 500

---

[3] *Indian Labour Year Book, 1974* (Simla: Labour Bureau, Ministry of Labour, Government of India, 1977), pp. 251-252.

[4] G. P. Sinha and P. R. N. Sinha, *Industrial Relations and Labour Legislation* (New Delhi: Oxford & IBH, 1977), p. 465.

[5] *Indian Labour Year Book, 1974*, pp. 256-260.

per month. Persons employed in a managerial or administrative capacity, even if they are earning less than Rs. 500 per month, are not deemed to be "workmen" and are therefore outside the scope of this act.

The main provisions of the Industrial Disputes Act of 1947, as amended in 1976, relate to: (1) works committees, (2) conciliation and adjudication machinery, (3) strikes and lockouts, and (4) layoffs and retrenchment. A summary of these provisions is given below.

1. *Works Committees.* The act requires that a consultative body of the employers and workmen be established in every industrial organization having one hundred or more workers; the workers' representatives, who should be chosen from the organization under consideration, should be at least equal in number to the employer's representatives. Works committees are to serve as the first step toward resolution of any dispute between the employers and the workmen.

2. *Conciliation and Adjudication Machinery*

A. *Conciliation and Courts of Inquiry.* The act provides for conciliation officers, boards of conciliation, and courts of inquiry for the settlement of industrial disputes. All disputes in public utility services are to be compulsorily referred for conciliation. Conciliation settlements are binding, and valid for six months unless otherwise provided. If conciliation fails, the appropriate authority shall submit the reasons thereof, along with recommendations for settlement of the dispute for adjudication, upon its discretion. In case of petitioning by either party in the dispute, the government is required to refer the dispute to a board, court, tribunal, or national tribunal.

B. *Adjudication.* A three-tier system of original tribunals, consisting of labor courts, industrial tribunals, and national tribunals, is provided by the act. Both state and central governments can appoint labor courts or industrial tribunals, but only the central government can appoint a national tribunal. The second and third schedules of the act detail the matters within the jurisdiction of the labor courts and the national tribunals, respectively. The second schedule covers day to day matters such as legality of orders passed by employers and dismissal of workmen, while the third schedule covers matters relating to wages, rationalization, closure, etc. Industrial tribunals are also empowered, in some cases, to cover matters detailed in the second schedule. The national tribunals are to adjudicate on matters referred by the government, which may cover issues of national importance or issues with implications in more than one state.

C. *Duration and Enforceability of Awards.* The normal period of existence of an award is one year; this may be extended by the government for a period not exceeding one year at a time, for a total of three years from the date of the initial award. The awards continue to be in operation even after the expiration date unless either party gives two months' notice of termination. The government has various powers to reduce the term of the award, or to modify it, based on certain circumstances, and upon following certain procedures of notification laid out in the act.

D. *Arbitration.* While the original act of 1947 did not provide for arbitration, subsequent amendments have introduced the process of arbitration as an alternative to which the parties to the dispute may take recourse, upon a written agreement to that effect and before the process of adjudication.

E. *Position During Pendency of Proceedings.* An amendment made to the act in 1956 provides that the applicable standing orders govern proceedings against any workman when an employer desires to proceed against him. In cases involving dismissal or discharge, one months' wages must be paid and approval should be sought from the appropriate authority. Certain worker representatives, however, are protected in all matters connected with the dispute or otherwise.

F. *Notice of Change.* No changes in the conditions of service applicable to any workman may be made without at least twenty-one days' notice.

G. *Penalties.* No distinction is made between first and subsequent conditions. Up to six months of imprisonment, or a fine, or both, may be awarded for noncompliance. Partial payment of the fine may be made to the aggrieved party as compensation. Penalties are also prescribed for other offenses such as illegal strikes and lockouts and disclosures of confidential information.

3. *Strikes and Lockouts.* The government may prohibit a strike or lockout if the dispute has already been referred to a board or tribunal. A strike in public utilities may be declared illegal if it is declared without adequate notice or during the period for which a settlement of award is in operation regarding the dispute, or if the dispute is under arbitration or adjudication. A strike or lockout, however, is considered legal if it commences before a dispute is referred for settlement. Further, a strike in response to an illegal lockout, or vice versa, is considered legal. Financial assistance in direct support of a strike is prohibited.

4. *Layoffs and Retrenchment.* The act provides for layoff and retrenchment compensation based on certain conditions. Any establishment having an average daily employment of fifty or more workers and where the work is not of an intermittent character is to pay layoff compensation to any worker who has had at least 240 days of service in the preceding twelve calendar months (190 days in the case of mine workers). Casual workers are excluded from this provision. The compensation is to be 50 percent of the basic wages plus the dearness allowance for all the days of layoff. The maximum period for compensation is forty-five days (provided that an agreement to that effect exists), after which the worker may be retrenched at any time by giving a one-month notice. The layoff compensation may be set off against the retrenchment compensation.

A laid-off workman may not be entitled to compensation if he refuses to accept alternative employment in the same or a nearby establishment, or if he is responsible for a strike or slowing-down of production. Workmen in the category eligible for layoff compensation are also eligible for retrenchment compensation. At least a one-month notice of retrenchment is to be given for any employee whose period of service has been at least one year: the government is to be notified of all cases of retrenchment. Retrenchment compensation is provided at the rate of fifteen days' average pay for each year of service. The general rule for retrenchment is to be "last come, first go."

The act provides that retrenchment compensation is payable in the event of closure or transfer of an undertaking and, under certain conditions, in the event of a change of ownership. In cases of closure due to causes beyond the control of employers, the maximum compensation has been limited to the average pay for three months.

Under the act as amended in 1976, no layoff or retrenchment is to be done in any establishment employing 300 or more workmen unless prior permission has been obtained, or without either giving at least a three-month notice or paying wages for the period of notice.

The Industrial Disputes Act of 1947 covers some of the most important issues relating to industrial relations. It seeks to protect the interests of both the workers and the employers. It is invoked often, even though bureaucratic delays and lack of proper enforcement have reduced its effectiveness.

The Industrial Employment (Standing Orders) Act of 1946

First passed in 1946 and amended since then, this act seeks to regulate the conditions of recruitment, discharge, disciplinary action, holidays, and other facets of employment in industrial establishments with one hundred or more workers. This act requires that employers define the terms and conditions of service in their establishments in writing and have such information certified by appropriate labor authorities. These rules or "standing orders" cover such issues as classification of workmen, mode of transmitting terms and conditions of service to workmen, rules covering shifts, attendance, and punctuality, mode of obtaining leave, and requirements for entry to the premises. The rules also encompass wider areas such as termination of employment, suspension or dismissal for misconduct, and means of redress for workmen. These rules can be interpreted as terms of an employment contract between the employer and the workers, with some important issues such as wages and benefits excluded. They are not subject to direct negotiations between the union and the employer. These parties may, however, enter into special terms of employment that are not in conflict with the "standing orders." [6]

The act provides "model" Standing Orders, which each establishment may use as a reference for framing its own set of rules. The orders pertaining to termination of employment are given in Appendix G.

---

[6] S. N. Misra, *Labour and Industrial Laws* (Allahabad: Allahabad Law Agency, 1978), pp. 191-192.

OTHER LABOR LAWS

In addition to the laws discussed above, several other important acts of legislation have been passed, focusing on issues such as wages, social security, safety, and welfare. These are discussed below.

Wage and Bonus Legislation

The payment of wages is governed by the Payment of Wages Act of 1936, and by the Minimum Wages Act of 1948, as amended subsequently. The Payment of Wages (Amendment) Act, 1976, extends to all of India and applies to persons employed in any factory as defined in the Factories Act of 1948, or by any railroad, and receiving wages and salaries which average below Rs. 1,000 per month. The act provides for payment of wages, after obtaining the written permission of the employee, either by check or by crediting his bank account.

Employers cannot withhold the wages earned by workers, nor can they make any unauthorized deductions. Industrial establishments employing less than 1,000 workers must pay wages before the expiry of the seventh day, and in other cases, before the expiry of the tenth day after the last day of the wage period. Fines can be imposed only for those acts approved by the appropriate government as acts of omission, and they must not exceed 3 percent of the wage payable. Fines cannot be recovered in installments or after the expiry of sixty days from the day of the act of omission for which the fine is imposed. If the payment of wages is delayed or if wrongful deductions are made, the workers or their trade unions can file claim. The payment of overtime in scheduled employments is governed by the Minimum Wages Act of 1948.

Employers in India are free to hire an employee on any terms that the employee will accept. The Minimum Wages Act of 1948, however, seeks to prevent the exploitation of labor. It also empowers the appropriate government, either central or state, to fix minimum wages of employees working in industries specified in the schedule. Wage rates in these industries have been fixed for various types of employment.

The act also provides for revision at suitable intervals of minimum wages that have already been fixed. Recently, minimum wages have been revised for workers in scheduled employment, agriculture, and various classes of mines.

Through an ordinance passed on September 26, 1975, which became an act on February 11, 1976, equal remuneration was assured to men and women workers throughout the country for the same work or work of similar nature. Discrimination against women in the matter of employment is prevented except for work in which the employment of women is prohibited or restricted by or under any law in force.

A compulsory bonus is paid to workers covered under the Payment of Bonus Act of 1965, which is applicable to every factory and establishment in which twenty or more persons are employed on any day during the accounting year. Employers are required to pay a minimum bonus regardless of profits. The current bonus laws provide for a minimum bonus of 8.33 percent, payable each year. The maximum bonus is 20 percent.

Social Security Legislation

India's social security legislation covers such important issues as compensation for accidental disability and death, medical insurance, provident funds and pensions, and maternity benefits. The specific risks and the laws under which they are covered are given in Table V-2.

The Workmen's Compensation Act of 1923, as amended in 1962, applies to workers earning less than Rs. 500 per month who are

TABLE V-2

Risks Covered Under Social Security Laws in India

Risk	Laws Under Which Covered
1. Disablement	a. Workmen's Compensation Act, 1923 b. Employees' State Insurance Act, 1948
2. Death	a. Workmen's Compensation Act, 1923 b. Employees' State Insurance Act, 1948
3. Maternity	a. State Maternity Benefit Acts b. Central Maternity Benefit c. Employees' State Insurance Act, 1948
4. Sickness	a. Employees' State Insurance Act, 1948
5. Old Age	a. Coal Mines Provident Fund and Bonus Scheme Act, 1948 b. Employees' Provident Funds Act, 1952 c. Assam Tea Plantations Provident Fund Scheme Act, 1955 d. Seamen's Provident Fund Act, 1966

Source: G. P. Sinha and P. R. N. Sinha, *Industrial Relations and Labour Legislation* (New Delhi: Oxford and IBH, 1977), p. 558.

employed in factories, mines, plantations, transport and construction work, railways, and other specified industries. The act does not apply to areas covered under the Employees' State Insurance Scheme, which is discussed later in this section, as disablement benefits for those workers are provided under the Employees' State Insurance Act.

The Workmen's Compensation Act provides for payment of compensation by employers to workmen or to their dependents, as applicable, in cases of injury, disease, or death arising in the course of employment. The amount of compensation depends on the nature of injury, and on the wage level of the worker. The minimum compensation for death is Rs. 1,000 and the maximum is Rs. 10,000. Compensation for disablement varies from a minimum of Rs. 1,400 to a maximum of Rs. 14,000. Compensation is payable in lump sum.[7]

The Employees' State Insurance Act of 1948 is designed to provide cash benefits in the case of illness, maternity, and injury, and payment in the form of pension to the dependents of workers who die of injury attained as a result of employment. This act introduced the contributory principle, under which both the employer and the employee are required to make contributions. The employee's contribution is to be deducted from his wages by the principal employer. The act also introduced protection against sickness, replaced lump-sum payments by pensions in the case of benefits to dependents, and placed the liability of claims on a statutory corporation, The Employees' State Insurance Corporation, to which the contributions of the workers and the employers are paid. This act and the Workmen's Compensation Act of 1923 have the same function, and the Employees' State Insurance Act is gradually replacing the Compensation Act. Benefits cannot be claimed under both the acts, and similarly, the employer's liability is limited to the law that is applicable to his establishment.

The Employees' Provident Fund and Family Pension Fund Act of 1952 and the Coal Mines Provident Fund, Family Pension, and Bonus Act of 1948 provide for the institution of compulsory provident funds for employees in factories, mines, and other establishments. Benefits to the dependents of the employees in cases of early death are also provided. The Employees' Provident Fund and Pension Fund Act applies to all establishments with twenty or more employees, with a few exceptions. Under the act, the

---

[7] *Report of the National Commission on Labour* (New Delhi: Ministry of Labour, Employment, and Rehabilitation, 1969), pp. 164-165.

employee is to make a contribution of 6¼ to 8 percent of his basic wages, depending on applicable classification, and the employer is required to make an equal contribution. The amount comprised of the employer's and the employee's contribution is to be credited to the Employees' Provident Fund account which is held by a prescribed bank. The Employees' Provident Fund Scheme covers all workers who have completed one year of continuous service or who have worked for 240 days during a period of 12 months and whose total wages or salary do not exceed Rs. 1000.00 per month.[8] Exemptions from the act can be granted to establishments that have private schemes whose terms are not less favorable than the statutory scheme. The law also provides for regulation of the provident fund accounts and requires that a legally prescribed interest be paid on the outstanding balances of each member's account.

Under the scheme, the full contribution made by an employee is to be paid to him, along with the employer's contribution and remaining interest on that amount at the time of the employee's retirement. In case of early retirement or separation from the establishment, the employer is required to pay the employee his contribution plus a percentage of the employer's contribution, which varies with the length of the employee's service. The employer's full contribution is paid to the employee in the event of permanent disability and to his dependents in the event of his death.

The act also provides for the long-term protection of the family of a worker who is a member of the Employees' Provident Fund Scheme and who dies prematurely in service of the employer. Under the act, the Employees Family Pension Scheme provides a pension ranging from Rs. 40 to Rs. 150 per month to the family of a member who dies while in service to the employer. The employee, however, must have been a member of the Provident Fund Scheme for at least two years in order to be eligible for this protection. Under the scheme, an eligible employee receives a retirement benefit of Rs. 4,000.[9]

The benefits available under the various social security laws in India are shown in Table V-3.

---

[8] *Indian Labour Year Book, 1974*, pp. 241-242.

[9] *Ibid.*, p. 245.

TABLE V-3

Benefits Under Social Security Laws in India

Topic	Benefits *	Relevant Law **
Sickness & Medical Care	Periodic cash payment to equal "daily standard benefit rate" fixed under the act (which is approximately equal to 50 percent of the average daily wages) up to a maximum of 56 days. Employees insured under the act can be granted up to 309 days sickness benefits if they contract a disease specified under the act.	The Employees' State Insurance Act, 1948
	Medical care for the employee and his family (where such benefit is extended to the family) in the form of out-patient treatment or in-patient admittance in a hospital or visits by an authorized physician to the home of the insured person.	The Employees' State Insurance Act, 1948
Maternity	Periodic cash payment in case of confinement or miscarriage or sickness arising out of pregnancy, premature birth of a child, or miscarriage equal to twice the standard benefits as prescribed by the act for a maximum period of 12 weeks.	The Employees' State Insurance Act, 1948
	In establishments where the Employees' State Insurance Act, 1948, does not apply, periodic cash payment equal to the worker's average daily wage for a maximum period of 12 weeks.	The Central Maternity Benefit Act, 1961
Disablement	Payment of a sum fixed by the law, which varies with the average monthly wages of the worker concerned, for injuries caused by accident arising out of and in the course of employment. This sum ranges from Rs. 1,400 to Rs. 14,000 for permanent total disablement and for permanent partial disablement and compensation is calculated on	The Workmen's Compensation Act, 1923

the basis of percentage loss of earning capacity. A half-monthly payment to be made in case of temporary disablement as prescribed by the law.

The Employees' State Insurance Act, 1948

125 percent of "daily standard benefit rate," which varies with the average wage, as fixed under the act, in case of temporary disablement. For permanent partial disablement the compensation is paid according to percentage loss of earning capacity. For permanent total disablement compensation is 125 percent of standard benefit rate. The compensation is payable for the entire duration of disablement and includes certain occupational diseases specified in the act. Payment is to be made periodically.

Retirement

Payment of an amount equal to the accumulated contribution in each employee's Provident Fund account. This includes both worker's and employer's contribution. The minimum contribution is prescribed by the act.

The Employees' Provident Fund and Family Pension Fund Act, 1952

The Coal Mines Provident Fund, Family Pension, and Bonus Schemes Act, 1948

Survivor's Benefits

Payment of compensation to dependent for death caused by accident arising out and in the course of employment equal to a sum fixed under the law. This sum ranges from Rs. 1,000 to Rs. 10,000 depending on the worker's wage group.

The Workmen's Compensation Act, 1923

Periodic payment to dependents equal to 125 percent of daily standard benefit rate for death of a worker due to an employment injury. Three-fifths payable to widow during her life or until remarriage. Two-fifths distributed equally to sons and daughters till the sons reach the age of eighteen or until the daughters marry or reach the age of eighteen, whichever is earlier.

The Employees' State Insurance Act, 1948

TABLE V-3 (Continued)

Topic	Benefit*	Relevant Law**
	Family Pension ranging from Rs. 40 to Rs. 70 per month to dependents of a worker who is a member of the Family Pension Scheme in case of the worker's death while in service. Also the payment of the accumulated Provident Fund balance in the worker's account is to be paid to the nominated dependent.	The Employees' Provident Fund and Family Pension Fund Act, 1952

* Not more than one benefit can be claimed in the same category.

** The laws are exclusive in that an establishment covered by one law is not covered by the others for the same benefit.

Source: *Indian Labour Year Book, 1974, passim.*

Safety and Welfare Legislation

The main legislative acts governing the safety and health of workers are: the Factories Act, 1948; the Mines Act, 1952; the Plantations Labour Act, 1951; the Indian Railways Act, 1890; the Dock Workers (Regulation of Employment) Act, 1948; the Motor Transport Workers Act, 1961; and the State Acts on Shops and Commercial Establishments. While the scope of these acts is wide, their concentration is on issues of health and safety, hours of work, and leaves and holidays, each dealing with a specific section of the Indian industry.

The Factories Act of 1948 specifies that workers cannot be required to work more than 48 hours a week or 9 hours in any day. The act prohibits employment of children below the age of 14 years, and requires that all workers between the ages of 14 and 18 be certified for fitness by a physician. Annual leave is required to be given to every employee who has worked for at least 240 days in a preceding calendar year at the rate of one day for every 20 days for adults and one day for every 15 days in the case of children.

The act requires compliance with the safety and welfare rules laid down in the law, which mainly relate to cleanliness, disposal of wastes and effluents, proper ventilation, control of temperature, elimination of dust and fumes, lighting, drinking water facilities, and sanitary facilities. It also provides for fencing of machinery, testing and examination of appliances and plant equipment, provision of safety equipment to workers, and fire prevention. The act requires that state and central governments enforce these laws and rules by providing inspections and imposing legal penalties for violation.[10]

The other acts prescribe similar measures for hours of work, leave, rest intervals, annual leave, and health and safety in various industrial sectors.

The Industrial Relations Bill of 1978

The multiplicity of labor legislation in India has been a cause of concern to trade unions, employers, and the government alike. The definition of "worker" varies in different laws; the applicability of each law and the interpretation of each have long been open to dispute. This problem can be solved only by having a compre-

---

[10] *Ibid.*, pp. 167-169.

hensive labor law which would replace the large number of individual laws in force and streamline the tripartite process of industrial relations between the government, trade unions, and employers. Following a recommendation of the National Tripartite Labour Conference held in May 1977, the government of India appointed a thirty-member tripartite committee. This committee was composed of representatives of all central workers' and employers' organizations and its purpose was to recommend a new comprehensive law on industrial relations.[11] Based on this committee's recommendation, the government submitted to the Parliament a comprehensive bill called the Industrial Relations Bill, 1978, for passage into law.

The Industrial Relations Bill, 1978, provided for the first time the determination of a "negotiating agent" with competence to negotiate with the management and enter into binding settlements. It also provided a procedure by which bipartite negotiations would be the first step in settling industrial disputes. A union can qualify as a "sole negotiating agent" if it enjoys support of at least 65 percent of employees and as "chief negotiating agent" if it has the support of at least 50 percent of the employees. The bill also sought to ban strikes and work stoppages in specified essential services, such as defense, airlines, and railways, and to impose penalties on both unions and management for violations of the law. It also stipulated that a strike in any establishment should not be conducted unless it is approved by at least 60 percent of the employees as ascertained in a secret ballot. The bill also sought to increase checks on layoffs, retrenchment, and closures, and to increase layoff compensation to the workers.[12]

The bill was strongly opposed by the trade union movement and supported by the employers. In face of this opposition, the bill was referred to a select committee and the government elected to seek a more balanced bill, taking into account objections raised by the trade unions. Because the government changed in January 1980, the original Industrial Relations Bill, 1978, is likely to be modified considerably before it is presented to Parliament again.

---

[11] *Social and Labour Bulletin* (Geneva: International Labour Office, 1978), No. 2/78, p. 123.

[12] "60% employees must back strike call," *The Economic Times,* August 30, 1978, p. 1.

LABOR ADMINISTRATION

The Ministry of Labor, government of India, is the central policy making, coordinating, controlling, and directing authority on labor issues. The Ministry of Labor has its main secretariat in New Delhi, with subordinate offices and statutory organizations elsewhere that administer programs and policies in particular areas.

A plethora of official entities exists in the area of industrial relations. The major ones include: the Office of the Chief Labour Commissioner, which administers the rules and laws regarding industrial disputes, settlements, and trade unions; the Labour Bureau, which collects, compiles, and publishes labor statistics required for the formulation of labor policy; the industrial tribunals and the labour courts, which deal with industrial disputes; and the Board of Arbitration, which is the apex arbitration authority. Others include the Office of the Director-General of the Employees' State Insurance Corporation, which administers the Employees' State Insurance Scheme. Finally, the Office of the Central Provident Fund Commissioner administers the Employees' Provident Fund and Family Pension Schemes.

Besides these central administrative offices, states have their own organizations for the administration and enforcement of the various labor laws in force within their territories.

CHAPTER VI

Conclusion

The year 1981 saw a gradual strengthening of the political and economic climate in India. Mrs. Gandhi now appears to have a focus and a determination that were clearly lacking one year ago. Economic pragmatism has to some extent taken precedence over political ideology; this can be clearly seen in the relaxation of restrictions on foreign companies operating in India, and in the shift in economic policy toward free enterprise. In fact, India has been seeking more commercial loans, and recently obtained a 5.7 billion dollar loan from the International Monetary Fund (IMF). The conditionalities imposed by the IMF on this loan have redirected the country toward free market philosophies, and the overall investment climate appears favorable.

Political pressures from "old guard" politicians who built their careers around the concept of "a socialistic pattern of society" are not likely to disappear and this may well lead to power struggles between various political segments in India. Mrs. Gandhi will have to continue exercising strong control of these divisive tendencies in her party and the government. Facing a well-entrenched Mrs. Gandhi, and realizing that disunity was the cause of their political debacle in the 1980 elections, many opposition parties have made moves toward coordinating their activities. While the strength of these moves is yet to be tested, they could prove to be a challenge to Mrs. Gandhi in the coming years.

Recent political tensions in Northeast India have accentuated the need for a more equitable distribution of political and economic power between central and state governments. The strong federal nature of the country has prevented this from happening so far, but a slight easing of this control may be necessary to avoid large-scale disturbances in the states.

The trade union movement, although suffering badly from fragmentation in its ranks, organized a one-day nationwide strike in January 1982 to press for the removal of restrictive labor laws and for greater economic benefits. The strike was by and large unsuccessful, not only because of strong countervailing measures taken by the government, but also because of the lack of unity of purpose among the various trade union factions. Such unity appears essential to the achievement of some progress toward the goal of better wages and increased social security and employment of the working class.

A tripartite conference between the government, employers, and the trade unions was proposed some time ago, and such an effort, combined with the move toward comprehensive industrial relations legislation, is likely to result in a more balanced version of the Industrial Relations Bill, 1978. This is particularly important if the decline in the industrial relations climate is to be reversed; the unions themselves will have to make efforts to train workers to increase their awareness of their rights and to generate union leadership from within the ranks of the labor force.

Despite social and economic problems, India appears set for political stability in a region in which instability is the norm. The recent shift to an economic policy more favorable to free enterprise, coupled with India's strong economic structure, is expected to improve substantially the investment climate. If the government opens its doors, even if selectively, to badly needed foreign investment, India has the potential of becoming one of the most attractive investment opportunities in South Asia. The fact that such a move seems to be approaching is an encouraging sign for India.

APPENDIXES

Appendix A

LIST OF INDUSTRIES EXEMPT FROM LICENSING

1. Small scale and ancillary units.

2. Undertakings involving investment (in land, building and machinery) of not more than Rs. 10 million.

3. Medium entrepreneurs for setting up industries listed below who do not require imported raw materials, imported capital goods or foreign collaboration:

    (1) Cotton spinning for the manufacture of cotton yarn up to a capacity of 50,000 spindles subject to the following provisions—a) the packings for hand-looms should be in accordance with the policy; b) no new unit should be less than 25,000 spindles; c) this relaxation is not applicable to units in large cities/metropolitan towns, (2) Solvent extraction of oil/oil cakes from minor seeds including cotton seeds, (3) Writing, printing and wrapping paper from agricultural residue and waste, (4) Rayon grade pulp from bamboo, (5) Refractories, (6) Water pumps beyond 10 cm. × 10 cm., (7) Cotton and linter pulp, (8) Tractor drawn agricultural implements, (9) Glass slag and mineral wool and products thereof, (10) Hard board including fibreboard/chipboard and the like, (11) GLS lamps, (12) Industrial sewing machines, (13) Basic drugs, (14) Forged hand tools and small tools, (15) Leather goods except those reserved for small scale industries, (16) Industrial machinery, (17) Surgical and medicinal rubber products, (18) LT Switchgear, (19) Machine Tools, (20) Industrial and scientific instruments, and (21) Basic insecticides.

4. Items of manufacture based on technology developed by National Laboratories/Institutions (this exemption is not available for items reserved for public or small scale sector or covered by special regulation. Undertakings under the pur-

view of MRTP Act or Foreign Exchange Regulation Act will also not be eligible for this exemption).

However, in respect of the following industrial undertakings, whether or not covered under 1, 2 and 3 above, an industrial license will be required irrespective of the quantum of capital outlay:

1. Undertakings in respect of which the additional investment along with the original investment exceeds Rs. 50 million.

2. Undertakings covered by Section 20(a) of the Monopolies and Retrictive Trade Practices (MRTP) Act 1969, i.e. undertakings whose own assets or whose own assets along with the assets of inter-connected undertakings are not less than Rs. 200 million.

3. Dominant undertakings covered by Section 20(b) of the MRTP Act 1969.

4. Undertakings belonging to "foreign concerns."

5. Undertakings which relate to the following categories of industries:

   (a) Industries listed in Schedule A of the Industrial Policy Resolution 1954, i.e., industries like Iron and Steel, Mineral Oils, Arms and Ammunition, etc., in which all new units would be set up exclusively by the State.

   (b) Specified industries subject to special regulation, viz., Coal, Textiles (including those dyed, printed or otherwise processed) manufactured, produced or processed on powerlooms; Milk foods; Malted foods, Roller Flour Milling; Oil Seed Crushing; Vanaspathi, Leather, Matches and Beer.

   (c) Other specified industries, viz., manufacture of all qualities of steel from electric furnaces based on scrap; Iron and steel pipes and tubes and stainless tubes; Bright bars; Tin containers and metal containers; Drums and barrels; Wires of mild steel, special steel and alloy steel-coated and uncoated; Hot-rolled bars/rods/sections or cold rolled steel strips and box strappings; Non-ferrous semis, alloys, flat products and extrusions excluding aluminum semis; Plastic processed goods; Industrial gases; steel forgings; AAC/ACSR conductors and Formaldehyde.

    (d) Items reserved for production in the small-scale sector (list of items currently so reserved is available on request).

6. An undertaking which requires foreign exchange in excess of any of the following limits:

    (a) 5 per cent of the ex-factory value of annual production or Rs. 0.5 million whichever is less for the import of raw materials (other than steel and aluminum) used in the manufacturing activity in any year.

    (b) 10 per cent of the ex-factory value of annual production or Rs. 0.5 million whichever is less in any year after three years of the commencement of production for the import of components used in the manufacturing activity.

Source: *Guide to Investing & Licensing in India* (New York: Indian Investment Centre), pp. 5-7.

Appendix B

INDUSTRIES IN WHICH LARGE-SCALE UNDERTAKINGS ARE PERMITTED (INDUSTRIAL LICENSING POLICY, FEBRUARY 1973)

1. Metallurgical Industries:
   (1) Ferro Alloys
   (2) Steel castings and forgings
   (3) Special steels
   (4) Non-ferrous metals and their alloys

2. Boilers and steam generating plants

3. Prime movers (other than electrical generators):
   (1) Industrial turbines
   (2) Internal combustion engines

4. Electrical equipment:
   (1) Equipment for transmission and distribution of electricity
   (2) Electric motors
   (3) Electrical furnaces
   (4) X-ray equipment
   (5) Electronic components and equipment

5. Transportation:
   (1) Mechanised sailing vessels up to 1000 DWT
   (2) Ship ancillaries
   (3) Commercial vehicles

6. Industrial machinery

7. Machine tools

8. Agricultural machinery: Tractors and power tillers

9. Earthmoving machinery

10. Industrial instruments: indicating, recording and regulating devices for pressure, temperature, rate of flow, weights, levels and the like

11. Scientific instruments

12. Nitrogenous and phosphatic fertilisers falling under '(1) Inorganic fertilisers' under '18. Fertilisers' in the First Schedule to the ID&R Act, 1951.

13. Chemicals (other than fertilisers):
   (1) Inorganic heavy chemicals
   (2) Organic heavy chemicals
   (3) Fine chemicals, including photographic chemicals
   (4) Synthetic resins and plastics
   (5) Synthetic rubbers
   (6) Man-made fibres
   (7) Industrial explosives
   (8) Insecticides, fungicides, weedicides and the like
   (9) Synthetic detergents
   (10) Miscellaneous chemicals (for industrial use only)

14. Drugs and Pharmaceuticals

15. Paper and pulp including paper products

16. Automobile tyres and tubes

17. Plate glass

18. Ceramics:
   (1) Refractories
   (2) Furnace lining bricks—acidic, basic and neutral

19. Cement products:
   (1) Portland cement
   (2) Asbestos cement

Note:—The classification of industries follows the First Schedule to the Industries (Development and Regulation) Act, 1951. Items of manufacture reserved for the public sector under Schedule A to the Industrial Policy Resolution, 1956 or for production in the small scale sector as may be notified from time to time will be excluded from the application of the list).

Source: *Guide to Investing & Licensing in India*, p. 9.

Appendix C

LIST OF INDUSTRIES IN WHICH FOREIGN COLLABORATION IS NOT CONSIDERED NECESSARY

1. Metallurgical industries:

Ferrous: ordinary castings, bright bars, structurals, welded OI steel pipes and tubes.

Non-ferrous: antimony, sodium metal, electrical resistance heating (nickel-free alloy), aluminium litho plates.

2. Electrical equipment: Electrical fans, common domestic appliances, common types of winding wires and strips, iron clad switches, AC motors, cables and distribution transformers.

3. Electronic components and equipments: General purpose transistors and diodes, paper, mica and variable capacitors, TV receivers, tape recorders, teleprinters, P. A. systems, record players/changers.

4. Scientific and industrial instruments: Non-specialised types of valves, meters, weighing machinery, and mathematical, surveying and drawing instruments.

5. Transportation: Railway wagons, bicycles.

6. Industrial machinery: Building and constructional machinery, oil mill machinery, conventional rice mill machinery, sugar machinery, tea processing machinery, general purpose machinery.

7. Machine tools: Forged hand tools, general purpose machine tools.

8. Agricultural machinery: Tractor drawn implements, power tillers, food grain dryers, agricultural implements.

9. Miscellaneous mechanical engineering industries.

10. Commercial, office and household equipments of common use.

11. Medical and surgical appliances.

12. Fertilizers: Single super phosphate, granulated fertilizers.

13. Chemicals (other than fertilizers) : acetic acid; acetanilide, ethyl chloride, viscose filament, yarn staple fibre, melathion technical, sulphate of alumina, potassium chlorate, fatty acid and glycerine, butyl titanate, warfarin, silica gel, lindene, endosulfan, phanthoate, nitrofen, ethyl ether, plastipeel.

14. Dyestuffs: Benzidine, o-toludine, carbozole dioxazine violet pigment, cadmium sulphide orange.

15. Drugs and pharmaceuticals: Caffeine (natural), phyenyl butazone, tol butamide, para acetamel, phanacetin, senna extract, diasogenin, clofibrate, 4-hydroxy cumarin, xenthopotoxin, calcium gluconate, choline chloride, glyceryl gualocolate, phenylethyl biguanide hydrochloride, scopolamine hydro-bromide, niacinamide, ortholelyl biguanide, colchicine, diazepam, sorbitol from dextrose monohydrate, berberine hydrochloride, belladonna, acriflavine, calcium hypophosphite, chlordiazepoxide.

16. Paper and pulp including paper products.

17. Consumer goods.

18. Vegetable oils and vanaspati.

19. Rubber industries: Viscose tyre yarn, metal bounded rubber, latex foam, rubberised fabrics, bicycle tyres and tubes.

20. Leather, leather goods and pickers; Belting-leather, cotton and hair finished leather, pickers, picking bands, vegetable tanning extracts, fat liquors other than synthetic.

21. Glass and ceramics.

22. Cement and gypsum products.

Note: The list is illustrative and not exhaustive. Clarification of details within the broad headings is the responsibility of administrative ministries.

Source: *The Economic Times*, Bombay, December 29, 1978, p. 1.

Appendix D

ILO CONVENTIONS RATIFIED BY INDIA AND THE DATES OF REGISTRATION OF THEIR RATIFICATION

Title of Convention	Date of registration of ratification
1. No. 1 Hours of Work (Industry), Convention, 1919	14-7-1921
*2. No. 2 Unemployment Convention, 1919	14-7-1921
3. No. 4 Night Work (Women) Convention, 1919	14-7-1921
4. No. 5 Minimum Age (Industry) Convention, 1919	9-9-1955
5. No. 6 Night Work of Young Persons (Industry) Convention, 1919	14-7-1921
6. No. 11 Right of Association (Agriculture) Convention, 1921	11-5-1923
7. No. 14 Weekly Rest (Industry) Convention, 1921	11-5-1923
8. No. 15 Minimum Age (Trimmers and Stokers) Convention, 1921	20-11-1922
9. No. 16 Medical Examination of Young Persons (Sea) Convention, 1921	20-11-1922
10. No. 18 Workmen's Compensation (Occupational Diseases) Convention, 1925	30-9-1927
11. No. 19 Equality of Treatment (Accident Compensation) Convention, 1925	30-9-1927
12. No. 21 Inspection of Emigrant Convention, 1926	14-1-1928
13. No. 22 Seamen's Articles of Agreement Convention, 1928	31-10-1932
14. No. 26 Minimum-Wage Fixing Machinery Convention, 1928	10-1-1955
15. No. 27 Marking of Weight (Packages Transported by Vessels) Convention, 1929	7-9-1931
16. No. 29 Forced Labour Convention, 1930	30-11-1954
17. No. 32 Protection Against Accidents (Dockers) Convention (Revised), 1932	10-2-1947
18. No. 41 Night Work (Women) Convention (Revised), 1934	22-11-1935
19. No. 45 Underground Work (Women) Convention, 1935	25-3-1938
20. No. 80 Final Articles Revision Convention, 1946	17-11-47
21. No. 81 Labour Inspection Convention, 1947	7-4-1949
22. No. 88 Employment Service Convention, 1948	24-6-1959

Title of Convention	Date of registration of ratification
23. No. 89 Night Work (Women) Convention (Revised), 1948	27-2-1950
24. No. 90 Night Work of Young Persons (Industry) Convention (Revised), 1948	27-2-1950
25. No. 100 Equal Remuneration Convention, 1951	25-9-1958
26. No. 107 Indigenous and Tribal Populations Convention, 1957	29-9-1958
27. No. 111 Discrimination (Employment and Occupation) Convention, 1958	3-6-1960
28. No. 116 Final Articles Revision Convention, 1961	22-6-1962
29. No. 42 Workmen's Compensation (Occupational Diseases) Convention (Revised), 1934	13-1-1964
30. No. 118 Equality of Treatment (Social Security) Convention, 1962	19-8-1964

* Ratification since denounced.

Source: *Indian Labour Year Book, 1974* (Labour Bureau, Ministry of Labour, Government of India, 1974), p. 292; and Industrial Research Unit files.

Appendix E

ILO RECOMMENDATIONS WHICH HAVE BEEN FULLY IMPLEMENTED BY INDIA

1. R. No. 2 —Reciprocity of Treatment.
2. R. No. 6 —White Phosphorus.
3. R. No. 9 —National Seamen's Codes.
4. R. No. 20 —Labour Inspection.
5. R. No. 24 —Workmen's Compensation (Occupational Diseases).
6. R. No. 25 —Equality of Treatment (Accident Compensation).
7. R. No. 28 —Labour Inspection (Seamen).
8. R. No. 30 —Minimum-Wage Fixing Machinery.
9. R. No. 34 —Protection against Accidents (Dockers) Consultation of Organizations.
10. R. No. 35 —Forced Labour (Indirect Compulsion).
11. R. No. 36 —Forced Labour (Regulation).
12. R. No. 40 —Protection against Accidents (Dockers) Reciprocity.
13. R. No. 48 —Seamen's Welfare in Ports.
14. R. No. 50 —Public Works (International Cooperation).
15. R. No. 68 —Social Security (Armed Forces).
16. R. No. 78 —Bedding, Mess Utensils and Miscellaneous Provisions (Ships Crews).
17. R. No. 81 —Labour Inspection.
18. R. No. 82 —Labour Inspection (Mining & Transport).
19. R. No. 90 —Equal Remuneration.
20. R. No. 92 —Voluntary Conciliation & Arbitration.
21. R. No. 94 —Cooperation at the Level of Undertaking.
22. R. No. 96 —Minimum Age (Coal Mines).
23. R. No. 102—Welfare Facilities.
24. R. No. 104—Indigenous & Tribal Populations.
25. R. No. 105—Ships' Medicine Chests.
26. R. No. 106—Medical Advice at Sea.
27. R. No. 107—Seafarers' Engagement (Foreign Vessels).
28. R. No. 108—Social Conditions & Safety (Seafarers).
29. R. No. 111—Discrimination (Employment and Occupation).
30. R. No. 113—Consultation (Industrial and National Levels).
31. R. No. 130—Examination of Grievances.

Source: *Indian Labour Year Book, 1974*, pp. 300-302; and Industrial Research Unit files.

Appendix F

LIST OF IMPORTANT LABOR LAWS

FACTORIES
CENTRAL

1. The Indian Boilers Act, 1923. Amended in 1929, 1937, 1939, 1942, 1943, 1947, 1949, 1951, 1952 and 1960.
2. The Cotton Ginning and Pressing Factories Act, 1925. Amended in 1939, 1942, 1950 and 1961.
3. The Factories Act, 1948. Amended in 1949 and 1954.

STATES

1. The Cotton Ginning and Pressing Factories (Bombay Amendment) Act, 1936. Amended in 1957.
2. C.P. & Berar Cotton Ginning and Pressing Factories (Amendment) Act, 1936 and 1947 @.
3. C.P. & Berar Cotton Ginning and Pressing Factories (Second Amendment) Act, 1947 @.
4. The Cotton Ginning and Pressing Factories (Madras Amendment) Act, 1953.
5. Cotton Ginning and Pressing Factories (Saurashtra Amendment) Act, 1956.

MINES
CENTRAL

1. The Mines Act, 1952.
2. The Mines (Amendment) Act, 1959.

3. The Metalliferous Mines Regulations, 1961. Amended in 1965 (Twice), 1966 and 1967.

STATES

1. The Bengal Mining Settlement Act, 1912.

PLANTATIONS
CENTRAL

1. The Tea Districts Emigrant Labour (Repeal), Act, 1970.
2. The Plantations Labour Act, 1951. Amended in 1953 and 1960.

STATES

1. The Jalpaiguri Labour Act, 1951.

TRANSPORT
CENTRAL

1. The Indian Railways Act, 1890. Amended in 1948, 1950, 1951, 1954, 1955, 1956 and 1957.
2. The Dock Workers (Regulations of Employment) Act, 1948. Amended in 1951, 1962 and 1970.
3. The Merchant Shipping Act, 1958. Amended in 1966.
4. The Motor Transport Workers Act, 1961.

SHOPS AND COMMERCIAL ESTABLISHMENTS
CENTRAL

1. The Weekly Holidays Act, 1942. Amended in 1951.

@ Not in force in Maharashtra.

* The Act has been brought into force with effect from 15th June, 1967.

** Schedule II to the Act was amended during 1966, 1967 and 1973 and a bill to further amend the Act was published in M. G. G. Part V on 3rd March, 1973.

STATES

1. The Andhra Pradesh Shops and Establishments Act, 1966 *. Amended in 1969.
2. The Assam Shops and Establishments Act, 1948.
3. The West Bengal Shops and Establishments Act, 1963 Amended in 1965.
4. The Bihar Shops and Establishments Act, 1953. Amended in 1959.
5. The Bombay Shops and Establishments Act, Act, 1948. Amended in 1949 and 1960 **.
6. The Delhi Shops and Establishments Act, 1954. Amended in 1960 and 1970.
7. The Jammu and Kashmir Shops and Establishments Act, 1966.
8. The Kerala Shops and Commercial Establishments Act, 1960.
9. The Madhya Pradesh Shops and Commercial Establishments Act, 1958. Amended in 1967.
10. The Madras Shops and Establishments Act, 1947. (Also applies to Andhra Pradesh with certain modifications).
11. The Madras Catering Establishments Act, 1958. Amended in 1961.
12. The Mysore Shops and Establishments Act, 1961.
13. The Orissa Shops and Commercial Establishments Act, 1956. Amended in 1958.
14. The Punjab Shops and Commercial Establishments Act, 1958.
15. The Rajasthan Shops and Commercial Establishments Act, 1958.
16. The Saurashtra Shops and Establishments Act, 1955.
17. The Uttar Pradesh Dookan Aur Vanijya Adhisthan Adhiniyam 1962.
18. The Pondicherry Shops and Establishments Act, 1964.
19. Himachal Pradesh Shops and Commercial Establishments Act, 1969.
20. H. P. Shops and Commercial Establishments Rules, 1972.
21. Maharashtra Grocery Markets Shops Unprotected Workers (Regulation of employment and welfare (i) amendment scheme 1973 and (ii) application to certain scheduled employments schemes).
22. A. P. Factories and Establishment (National Festivals and other holidays) Act, 1974 and Rules, 1974.
23. Goa, Daman and Diu Shops and Establishments Act, 1973.

WAGES AND BONUS

CENTRAL

1. The Payment of Wages Act, 1936. Amended in 1937, 1940, 1948, 1957, 1964.
2. The Minimum Wages Act, 1948. Amended in 1954, 1957 and 1961.
3. The Payment of Bonus Act, 1965. Amended in 1969, 1972 and in September and December, 1973 and in 1974.

STATES

1. The Payment of Wages (Bombay Amendment) Act, 1953.
2. The Payment of Wages (Bombay Amendment and Validation) Act, 1959.
3. The Payment of Wages (Madras Amendment) Act, 1957 and 1959.
4. The Payment of Wages (Mysore Amendment) Act, 1952.
5. The Payment of Wages (Saurashtra Amendment) Act, 1955.
6. The Minimum Wages (Rajasthan Amendment and Validation) Act, 1969.
7. The Payment of Wages (Madhya Pradesh Amendment) Act, 1964.

INDUSTRIAL HOUSING

1. The Bombay Housing Board Act, 1948. Amended in 1949, 1950, 1951, 1963 and 1964.
2. The Madhya Pradesh Housing Board Act, 1950.

3. The Uttar Pradesh Industrial Housing Board Act, 1950.

4. The Andhra Pradesh Housing Board Act, 1956.

5. The Punjab Industrial Housing Act, 1956.

6. The Mysore Housing Board Act, 1962.

7. The Assam State Housing Board Act, 1972.

SAFETY AND WELFARE

CENTRAL

1. The Indian Dock Labourers Act, 1934. Amended in 1950 and 1951.

2. The Mica Mines Labour Welfare Fund Act, 1946. Amended in 1950 and 1951.

3. The Coal Mines Labour Welfare Fund Act, 1947. Amended in 1951 and 1972.

4. The Coal Mines (Conservation and Safety) Act, 1952. Amended in 1961.

5. Iron Ore Mines Labour Welfare Cess Act, 1961. Amended in 1970.

6. The Lime Stone and Dolomite Mines Labour Welfare Fund Act, 1972.

STATES

1. The Bombay Smoke Nuisance Act, 1912. Amended in 1953.

2. The Bombay Labour Welfare Fund Act, 1953. Amended in 1956, 1961, 1966 and 1970.

3. The U.P. Sugar and Power Alcohol Industries Labour Welfare and Development Fund Act, 1950.

4. The U.P. Labour Welfare Fund Act, 1965.

5. The Mysore Labour Welfare Fund Act, 1965.

6. The Punjab Labour Welfare Fund Act, 1965.

7. The Maharashtra Mathadi, Hamal and other Manual Workers (Regulation of Employment and Welfare) Act, 1969. Amended in 1973.

8. Tamil Nadu Labour Welfare Fund Act, 1972.

9. The Assam Tea Plantations Employees' Welfare Act, 1959.

10. West Bengal Labour Welfare Fund Act, 1974.

11. Jammu & Kashmir Forest Labour Welfare and Common Facilities Fund Rules, 1974.

SOCIAL SECURITY

CENTRAL

1. The Workmen's Compensation Act, 1923. Amended in 1924, 1925, 1929, 1933, 1937 (Twice), 1938, 1939, 1942, 1946, 1948, 1959, 1962.

2. The Employers' Liability Act, 1938. Amended in 1951 and 1952.

3. The War Injuries Ordinance, 1941. Amended in 1950.

4. The War Injuries (Compensation Insurance) Act, 1943. Amended in 1960.

5. The Employees' State Insurance Act, 1948. Amended in 1951 and 1966.

6. The Coal Mines Provident Fund. Family Pension and Bonus Schemes Act, 1948. Amended in 1950, 1951, 1965, 1971 and 1972.

7. The Employees' Provident Funds and Family Pension Fund Act, 1952. Amended in 1953, 1956, 1958, 1960, 1962, 1963, 1965, 1971 and 1973.

8. The Maternity Benefit Act, 1961. Amended in 1972 and 1973.

9. The Personal Injuries (Emergency Provision) Act, 1962. Amended in 1971.

10. The Personal Injuries (Compensation Insurance) Act, 1963. Amended in 1971.

11. The Seamen's Provident Fund Act, 1966.

12. The Payment of Gratuity Act, 1972.

STATES

1. The Assam Maternity Benefit Act, 1944. Amended in 1951.

2. The Assam Tea Plantations Provident Fund Scheme Act, 1955.

3. The Bengal Rural and Unemployment Relief Act, 1939. Amended in 1941.
4. The Bengal (West) Maternity Benefit. (Tea Estates) Act, 1948. Amended in 1950 and 1959.
5. The Uttar Pradesh Maternity Benefit Act, 1938.
6. The West Bengal Employees' Payment of Compulsory Gratuity Act, 1971.
7. West Bengal E.S.I. (Medical Benefits) Rules, 1974.

INDUSTRIAL RELATIONS

CENTRAL

1. The Trade Unions Act, 1926. Amended in 1928, 1942, 1947, 1960 and 1964.
2. The Industrial Employment (Standing Orders) Act, 1946. Amended in 1950, 1951, 1961 and 1963.
3. The Industrial Disputes Act, 1947. Amended in 1948, 1949, 1950, 1951 (Thrice), 1952, 1953, 1954, 1955, 1956, 1957, 1964, 1965, 1971 and 1972.
4. The Industrial Disputes (Banking Companies) Decision Act, 1955. Amended in 1957 and 1972.
5. The Industrial Disputes (Banking and Insurance Companies) Act, 1949. Amended in 1952.
6. The Industrial Disputes (Appellate Tribunal Act, 1950. Amended in 1955.
7. The Industrial Disputes (Amendment and Miscellaneous Provisions) Act, 1956.
8. The Working Journalists (Conditions of Service and Miscellaneous Provisions) Act, 1955. Amended in 1962.
9. The Working Journalists (Fixation of Rates of Wages) Act, 1958. Amended in 1962.

STATES

1. The Bengal (West) Industrial Disputes (Amendment) Act, 1958. Amended in 1971 and 1973.
2. The Bihar Essential Services (Maintenance) Act, 1947.
3. The Industrial Disputes (Bihar Amendment) Act, 1959.
4. The Bombay Adjudication Proceedings (Transfer and Continuance) Act, 1947.
5. The Bombay Industrial Relations Act, 1946. Amended in 1948 (Thrice), 1949, 1953, 1955 and 1966.
6. Bombay Industrial Relations (Gujarat Extension and Amendment) Act, 1961. Amended in 1962 and 1964.
7. The Industrial Employment (Standing Orders) (Bombay Saurashtra Amendment) Act, 1953.
8. The Industrial Employment (Standing Orders) (Bombay Amendment) Act, 1955 and 1957.
9. The C.P. and Berar Validation of Awards and Continuance of Proceedings (Industrial Disputes) Act, 1947.
10. The C.P. and Berar Industrial Disputes Settlement Act, 1947. Amended in 1947, 1951 and 1955.
11. The Indian Trade Unions (Madhya Pradesh Amendment) Act, 1963.
12. The Trade Unions (Madhya Pradesh Amendment) Act, 1968.
13. The Madhya Pradesh Industrial Relations Act, 1960. Amended in 1965.
14. The Madhya Pradesh Industrial Employment (Standing Orders) Act, 1961. Amended in 1965.
15. The Industrial Disputes (Madras Amendment) Act, 1959.
16. The Industrial Employment (Standing Orders) (Madras Amendment) Act, 1960.
17. The Mysore Essential Services (Maintenance) Act, 1943.
18. The Industrial Disputes (Mysore Amendment) Act, 1953.
19. The Maharashtra Recognition of Trade Union and Prevention of Unfair Labour Practices Act, 1971.

20. The Mysore Industrial Disputes (Amendment and Repealing) Act, 1959.
21. The Mysore Labour (Administration) Act, 1952.
22. The Industrial Disputes (Orissa Amendment) Act, 1953.
23. The Industrial Disputes (Punjab Amendment) Act, 1958.
24. The Industrial Disputes (Rajasthan Amendment) Act, 1970.
25. The Industrial Disputes (Rajasthan Amendment) Ordinance, 1969.
26. The Industrial Disputes (Saurashtra Amendment) Act, 1953.
27. The U.P. Industrial Disputes Act, 1947. Amended in 1950, 1951 and 1953.
28. The U.P. Industrial Disputes (Amendment and Miscellaneous Provisions) Act, 1956. Amended in 1957.
29. Maharashtra Industrial Relations (Validations of certain Proceedings) Act, 1972.
30. Bombay Industrial Relations (Gujarat Amendment) Act, 1972.
31. Bombay Industrial Relations and Industrial Disputes (Gujarat Amendment) Act, 1972.
32. Industrial Disputes (Maharashtra) (Amendment) Act, 1973.

PROTECTION OF CHILDREN

CENTRAL

1. The Children (Pledging of Labour) Act, 1933.
2. The Employment of Children, Act, 1938. Amended in 1939, 1948, 1949 and 1951.

INDEBTEDNESS

STATES

1. The Assam Money Lenders' Act, 1934. Amended in 1954.
2. The Bengal Workmen's Protection Act, 1934. Amended in 1940.
3. The Bihar Workmen's Protection Act, 1948.

4. The Bombay Agricultural Debtors Relief Act, 1947.
5. The Bombay Money Lenders' Act, 1946. Amended in 1948.
6. The C.P. and Berar Adjustment and Liquidation of Industrial Workers Debt Act, 1936.
7. The C.P. Protection of Debtors Act, 1937.
8. The Agriculturists Loan (Coorg Amendment) Act, 1936.
9. The Coorg Debt Conciliation Act, 1940.
10. The Coorg Money Lenders' Act, 1939. Amended in 1946.
11. The Madras Debtors' Protection Act, 1934.
12. The Madras Workmen's Protection Act, 1941.
13. The Orissa Debt and Bondage Abolition Regulation, 1948.
14. The Punjab Registration of Accounts Act, 1930.
15. The Punjab Relief of Indebtedness Act, 1934.
16. The Punjab Debtors' Protection Act, 1936.
17. The Punjab Regulation of Money Lenders' Act, 1936.
18. The Saurashtra Agricultural Debtors' Relief Act, 1954.
19. Kerala Agricultural Workers Act, 1974.

MISCELLANEOUS

CENTRAL

1. The Cotton Industry (Statistics) Act, 1926. Amended in 1950.
2. The Employment Exchanges (Compulsory Notification of Vacancies) Act, 1959.
3. The Collection of Statistics Act, 1953.
4. The C.P.W.D. Contractors' Labour Regulations, 1946.
5. The Apprentices Act, 1961. Amended in 1972.
6. The Beedi and Cigar Workers' (Conditions of Employment) Act, 1966.

7. The Contract Labour (Regulation and Abolition) Act, 1970.

8. The Central Labour Laws (Extension to Jammu and Kashmir) Act, 1970.

9. Contract Labour (Regulation & Abolition) Rules, 1971—Construction and Maintenance of Creches.

10. Contract Labour (Regulation and Abolition) Act, 1970—Prohibition of Contract Labour in certain employments in coal mines.

11. Additional Emoluments (Compulsory Deposit Scheme) Act, 1974.

STATES

1. The Bombay Tenancy and Agricultural Lands Act, 1948.

2. The C.P. & Berar Regulation of Manufacture of Bidis (Agricultural Purposes) Act, 1948.

3. The Hyderabad Public Contractors' Labour Regulations and Fair Wage Clauses, 1951.

4. The Jammu and Kashmir Collection of Statistics Act, 1960.

5. The Kerala Industrial Establishments (National and Festival Holidays) Act, 1958.

6. The Madras Compulsory Labour Act, 1958.

7. The Madras Industrial Establishments (National and Festival Holidays) Act, 1958. Amended in 1964.

8. The Madras Beedi Industrial Premises (Regulations and Conditions of Work) Act, 1958.

9. The Orissa Compulsory Labour Act, 1948.

10. The Kerala Cigar and Beedi Industrial Premises (Regulations and Conditions of Work) Act, 1961.

11. The Pondicherry Industrial Establishments (National and Festival Holidays) Act, 1964. Amended in 1971.

12. The Punjab Industrial Establishments (National and Festival Holidays, Casual and Sick Leave) Act, 1965.

13. The U.P. Industrial Establishments (National Holidays) Act, 1961.

14. The Uttar Pradesh Industrial Undertakings (Special Provisions for Prevention of Unemployment) Act, 1966.

15. Bombay Lifts Act, 1939 as extended to the Province of Delhi.

16. The West Bengal Payment of Subsistence Allowance Act, 1969.

17. Himachal Pradesh, Industrial Establishments (National and Festival Holidays, Casual and Sick Leave) Act, 1969.

18. Contract Labour (Regulation & Abolition) Jammu & Kashmir Rules, 1972.

19. West Bengal Contract Labour (Regulation & Abolition) Rules, 1972.

20. Goa, Daman and Diu Contract Labour (Regulation and Abolition) Rules, 1972.

21. Andaman & Nicobar Islands Contract Labour (Regulation and Abolition) Rules, 1974.

22. Contract Labour (Regulation and Abolition) Karnataka Rules, 1974.

Source: *Indian Labour Year Book, 1974*, pp. 295-298.

Appendix G

MODEL STANDING ORDERS

Termination of Employment

Sec. 13. (1) For terminating employment of a permanent workman, notice in writing shall be given either by the employer or the workman—one month's notice in the case of monthly-rated workmen and two weeks' notice in the case of other workmen: one month's or two weeks' pay, as the case may be, may be paid in lieu of notice.

(2) No temporary workman whether monthly-rated, weekly-rated or piece-rated and no probationer or *badli* shall be entitled to any notice or pay in lieu thereof if his services are terminated, but the services of a temporary workman shall not be terminated as a punishment unless he has been given an opportunity of explaining the charges of misconduct alleged against him in the manner prescribed in paragraph 14.

(3) Where the employment of any workman is terminated, the wages earned by him and other dues, if any, shall be paid before the expiry of the second working day from the day on which his employment is terminated.

Disciplinary Action for Misconduct

Sec. 14. (1) A workman may be fined up to two per cent of his wages in a month for any of the following acts and omissions, namely:

(2) A workman may be suspended for a period not exceeding four days at a time, or dismissed without notice or any compensation in lieu of notice, if he is found to be guilty of misconduct.

(3) The following acts and omissions shall be treated as misconduct:

    (a) wilful insubordination or disobedience, whether alone or in combination with other, to any lawful and reasonable order of a superior,

(b) theft, fraud; or dishonesty in connection with the employ- ers' business or property,

(c) wilful damage to or loss of employers' goods or property,

(d) taking or giving bribes or any illegal gratification,

(e) habitual absence without leave or absence without leave for more than 10 days,

(f) habitual late attendance,

(g) habitual breach of any law applicable to the establishment,

(h) riotous or disorderly behavior during working hours at the establishment or any act subversive of discipline,

(i) habitual negligence or neglect of work,

(j) frequent repetition of any act or omission for which a fine may be imposed to a maximum of 2 per cent of the wages in a month,

(k) striking work or inciting others to strike work in contra- vention of the provisions of any law, or rule having the force of law.

(4) No order of dismissal shall be made unless the workman concerned is informed in writing of the alleged misconduct and is given an opportunity to explain the circumstances alleged against him. The approval of the manager of the establishment or where there is no manager, of the employer is required in every case of dismissal and, when circumstances appear to warrant it, the man- ager or the employer may institute independent enquiries before dealing with charges against a workman:

Provided that in the case of workmen to whom the provisions of Art. 311 of clause (2) of the Constitution of India apply, the provisions of that Article shall be complied with.

(5) An order of suspension shall be in writing and may take effect immediately on delivery to the workman. Such order shall set out in detail the alleged misconduct and the workman shall be given an opportunity of explaining the circumstances alleged against him. If on enquiry the order is confirmed, the workman shall be deemed to have been absent from duty for the period of suspension and shall not be entitled to any remuneration for such period. If, however, the order is rescinded, the workman shall be deemed to have been on duty during the period of suspension and shall be entitled to the same wages as he would have received if he had not been suspended.

(6) In awarding punishment under this standing order, the manager shall take into account the gravity of the misconduct, the previous record, if any, of the workman and any other extenuating or aggravating circumstances that may exist. A copy of the order passed by the manager shall be supplied to the workman concerned.

Source: Arjun P. Aggarwal, *Indian and American Labor Legislation and Practices* (New York: Asia Publishing House, 1966), pp. 228-230.

Index

ADMK. *See* Anna Dravid Munnetra
Kazhagam
Ahmedabad Mill Owners Association,
68, 70
AITUC. *See* All-India Trade Union
Congress
Akali Dal Party, 14
All-India Radio, 38
All-India Red Trade Union Congress,
71-72
merger with AITUC, 72
All-India Trade Union Congress
(AITUC), 68, 69, 71, 76, 78,
81, 82, 83, 85, 86, 90
description of, 69, 82-83
and WFTU, 90
Anna Dravid Munnetra Kazhagam
(ADMK), 14
balance of trade, 50
Bangladesh, 16
formation of, 7, 15
Bharat Heavy Electricals Ltd.
(BHEL), 48
Bharat Heavy Plates and Vessels Ltd.
(BHPV), 48
Bhartiya Janata Party (BJP), 12,
14, 84
formation of, 84-85
Bhartiya Kranti Dal (BKD), 12
Bhartiya Lok Dal (BLD), 12
Bhartiya Mazdoor Sangh (BMS), 84,
86
formation of, 84
BHEL. *See* Bharat Heavy Electricals
Ltd.
BHPV. *See* Bharat Heavy Plates and
Vessels Ltd.
BJP. *See* Bhartiya Janata Party
BLD. *See* Bhartiya Lok Dal
BKD. *See* Bhartiya Kranti Dal
BMS. *See* Bhartiya Mazdoor Sangh
Bombay Industrial Disputes Act of
1938, 74
Bombay Mill Hands Association, 68,
70
British Trade Union Congress, 98

Carter administration, 16-17
CENTO. *See* Central Treaty Organi-
zation
Central Treaty Organization
(CENTO), 16
Centre of Indian Trade Unions
(CITU), 83, 88
formation of, 84
China
border conflict with, in 1962, 4
relations with, 15
CITU. *See* Centre of Indian Trade
Unions
Coal India, Ltd., 40
Coal Mines Provident Fund, Family
Pension and Bonus Act of
1948, 108
Coca-Cola, 64
Code of Discipline, 78
commerce and trade, 49-57
principal trading partners of India, 50
Communist Party of India (CPI), 14,
82, 83
Communist Party of India/Marxist
(CPI/M), 14, 82-83
conciliation and adjudication machinery, 102
adjudication, 103-04
arbitration, 103
conciliation and courts of inquiry,
102
duration and enforceability of
awards, 103
notice of change, 103
penalties, 103-04
position during pendency of proceedings, 103
Congress Party, 9
under leadership of Indira Gandhi,
6-7
Congress (Indira) Party, 7, 8, 10
Congress (Organization) Party, 10
Congress (Ruling) Party, 10
Congress (Reddy) Party, 10
Congress (Urs) Party, 10

143

BY THE SAME AUTHOR

BIOGRAPHY, ETC.

RONSARD.

EMPEROR OF THE WEST.

FRANÇOIS VILLON: *A Documented Survey.*

* * *

THE ANATOMY OF DANDYISM.
  From the French of Barbey d'Aurevilly.
  Dry-points by Hermine David.

THE LONDON SPECTACLE, 1935.
  (Illust. Feliks Topolski.)

THE STUFFED OWL.
  An Anthology of Bad Verse (with Charles Lee).

A CHRISTMAS BOOK.
  (With G. C. Heseltine.)

* * *

DIVERSIONS.

AT THE SIGN OF THE BLUE MOON.

AT THE BLUE MOON AGAIN.

ON STRAW, AND OTHER CONCEITS.

WELCOME TO ALL THIS.

TAKE IT TO BED.

etc.

THE HOODED HAWK